Reviews

Have you ever wanted something so badly it was all you could think of? All you could talk about, write about, dream about. Claire did. She wanted a horse. Finding Heart Horse is her journey and her search for her Heart Horse. It takes her from being "the girl most likely to succeed" to a life on the streets of Yorkville in the late sixties.

As an adopted child she had no identity, no history, and no place where she "fit." Her years on the streets lead her into many dark places, where she began to add more secrets and traumas to her already large collection in the wall of secrets.

Life changed quickly in those days, from peace and love to war and violence. She went along for the ride not knowing where it would lead, just knowing that she had to find Heart Horse.

If you know anyone who may be struggling, perhaps even yourself, Finding Heart Horse can give you hope where you thought there was none. We all have different journeys, but the essence is the same. We all want to be loved, to belong, and to be happy. Everyone at some point has yearned for something so powerful that, like a magnet, it pulls you into the unknown. Even if you weren't really sure what it was for, you knew you had to pursue it.

Life lessons are learned, spirituality discovered. The reality of opposites is proven. With pain comes pleasure, with despair comes hope, with sadness comes joy, and perhaps along the way even your Heart Horse may be found.

This account of her adopted life by Claire Hitchon, the first of two memoirs, is a true story of courage, endurance, and survival in the face of abuse, hardship, and misfortune. She writes with clarity, never losing sight of her Heart Horse, the beauty of her future. This work by a new writer is encouraging, uplifting, and inspirational. Can't wait for the next book!

Von Coates
Adoption blogger, Activist and Post-Adoption Consultant

To not only live and survive this story once, but then to put a pen to paper to relive it again requires tremendous strength and courage. I am always in awe of the human spirit. The inner knowing that pulls you forward despite the odds, knowing there has to be something better.

Tammy Chater
Traditional Chinese Medicine RAc

A portion of the royalties from this book will be donated to Covenant House, Vancouver, Canada.

Finding Heart Horse

A MEMOIR OF SURVIVAL

CLAIRE HITCHON

With Janice Harper

First Prize Winner in the Hay House Nonfiction Contest 2013

BALBOA
PRESS
A DIVISION OF HAY HOUSE

Balboa Press books may be ordered through booksellers or by contacting:

Balboa Press
A Division of Hay House
1663 Liberty Drive
Bloomington, IN 47403
www.balboapress.com
1 (877) 407-4847

Because of the dynamic nature of the Internet, any web addresses or
links contained in this book may have changed since publication and
may no longer be valid. The views expressed in this work are solely those
of the author and do not necessarily reflect the views of the publisher,
and the publisher hereby disclaims any responsibility for them.

The author of this book does not dispense medical advice or prescribe the use
of any technique as a form of treatment for physical, emotional, or medical
problems without the advice of a physician, either directly or indirectly. The
intent of the author is only to offer information of a general nature to help
you in your quest for emotional and spiritual well-being. In the event you use
any of the information in this book for yourself, which is your constitutional
right, the author and the publisher assume no responsibility for your actions.

Any people depicted in stock imagery provided by Thinkstock are models,
and such images are being used for illustrative purposes only.
Certain stock imagery © Thinkstock.

Printed in the United States of America.

ISBN: 978-1-4525-8607-6 (sc)
ISBN: 978-1-4525-8609-0 (hc)
ISBN: 978-1-4525-8608-3 (e)
Library of Congress Control Number: 2013920233

Balboa Press rev. date: 12/9/2013

This book is dedicated to all beings that suffer.
May they find hope and discover resilience within themselves.

"With flowing tail and flying mane,
Wide nostrils never stretched by pain,
Mouths bloodless to the bit or rein,
And feet that iron never shod,
And flanks unscarred by spur or rod
A thousand horse, the wild and free,
Like waves that follow o're the sea,
Came thickly thundering on."

—Lord Byron, Mazeppa, 1819

Acknowledgments

This memoir was written in anticipation that my story will reach someone's heart and spark a flame of hope for that person to go on, find the resilience needed to survive, or thrive and live. I have learned a great deal in these six decades of life, and I want to acknowledge all of the teachers I've had, both formally and informally, and all those who helped me along the way.

There are no accidents in life—it is always a great teacher. Synchronicity played a part in bringing me to a medical conference where I met an author who kindly gave me the name of Janice Harper. Janice has been amazing in helping me sort out the many stories in one huge pile of writing and dividing it into two. Thank you.

Immense gratitude goes to the Dakini figures (female, energetic beings, spiritual muses, inspirational, wrathful figures in Tibetan Buddhism) that have played such a huge part in my ability to recognize what my life has meant and will mean as I move forward through these life stories.

Unending thanks and love goes to my first mentor (Dakini) Daryl.

I am so grateful to all the teachers of the Dharma that have come into my life with lessons to be learned, prayers to be said, and conversations to be had. Without them, I would never have been able to be here now, in peace.

To my dear friends, Susan Wilson, Catherine Leigh, Darlene Smith, Karen Baker and Diane Richards, who have stood by me throughout this healing process, my heart is yours.

To my friends Joan Carruthers, Bill Varela and John Ostrander, who were always close by to lend a helping hand when needed and offer words of encouragement, thank you.

Immense gratitude and love goes to Tammy Chater, who has travelled this writing journey with me, healing my body, mind and spirit in so many ways. I couldn't have done it without you.

To my amazing daughter, I hope when these books are completed that I will have inspired you as much as your presence in my life has inspired me. I love you always and forever.

This book is a compilation of memory, imagination, deduction, investigation, and supposition. It is an honest inquiry into my life, but my memory is my own. It is limited by the limits of my own mind and impacted by my perceptions. I have omitted some names, changed others, and left many as they are.

About a Horse

I always wanted a horse. I've wanted a wild horse, a Palomino horse, an Appaloosa horse, a racehorse, a pony horse, and even a miniature horse. I would have settled for a rocking horse, a stuffed horse, or even just a picture of a horse when I was a child, but even those small pleasures were prohibited. And so it was that when I was eight years old, I gave myself my own horse, my imaginary Heart Horse.

I've had this strong attraction to horses for as long as I can remember. Like a magnet, they have always pulled me in and held me close. They appear in my dreams and on blank pages in my sketchbook. They calm me when I'm disturbed and excite me when I'm bored. My nose longs to inhale their warmth, and my fingers crave the feel of their soft, wet nuzzle. My eyes are drawn into their own dark, all-knowing eyes, and I immediately feel an inexplicable connection. *This must be what it feels like to be loved,* I think whenever a horse looks into my eyes.

I never want to leave their safety, even when I know they are not real. But when they are real and standing there before me, it is all the more astounding. How can such a powerful animal be so gentle, and such a gentle beast so beautiful?

There is a magical essence I feel when I am with a horse. It's as if they know me and love me just the same. They see right into a person's soul and know immediately who they are and what they need.

A horse was the only thing I ever put on my Christmas list when I was a child. It was a huge request, I realized, when even the smallest desire was always denied. Gifts were considered indulgences that would only spoil a child, and toys were just distractions from my chores. When I received a gift from someone, it almost always disappeared, relegated to a hidden box to remain out of sight, or was given to another child who was considered more deserving.

But I never gave up my quest to find a horse of my own.

When my parents took me to visit my aunt and uncle who lived on a farm, I quickly and quietly made my way into the world of the barn where the horse's lived. I would nestle into the golden straw, inhaling the fragrant honey dust, as hours magically disappeared. Listening to an orchestra of barnyard sounds while enveloped in the dusty air brought me a perfect peace.

It was into that perfect peace that my Heart Horse first made his appearance.

Just as if he were a real horse, my Heart Horse danced and pranced and snorted with joy. Sometimes when he was afraid, I could feel him inside my own heart, racing around frantically, as if to warn me of pending danger. Other times he stood quietly in the grass, munching on crispy red apples and appearing deep in thought, as if to just let me know he was near. And sometimes he galloped wildly, free of restraint, tickling me with his unrestrained joy. But those happy and free rides were rare. Mostly he stood guard.

Old Uncle Willy understood my love of horses. He understood my connection to them and my ache to be closer to such a strangely forbidden desire. Uncle Willy always seemed to know where to look for me whenever we went to the farm. And he always seemed to know *to* look for me when others didn't.

One morning when I was huddled under a mountain of straw in the corner of Ginger's stall Uncle Willy came looking for me. He found me hiding there, buried under a pile of golden grass and crying, and Ginger standing over me with her warm breath tickling my neck, as if to say, "Everything will be okay."

I was hiding in there because my cousin had told me, yet again, that I wasn't real family. It seemed that each time she said that, it hurt a little bit more. Sometimes she even said it front of my mother, but instead of telling her to stop saying such awful lies, my mother would just agree. That really stung. And it made me sad.

I wasn't sure what they meant by not being "real" family—I was just as real as they were. After all, I had the pictures of my parents holding me when I was a newborn, teaching me piano when I was a toddler, and posing me in front of furniture, houses, or relatives. What could they possibly mean that I wasn't real family? I didn't understand at all, but I knew that there was something about me that was different. I just had no idea what it was.

Uncle Willy seemed to understand why I was crying, but he didn't ask me about it. Instead, he told me a story about the Rocky Mountains and the wild horses that lived there. With his soft and comforting words, my uncle told me all about how magnificent it was to see a thundering herd suddenly appear in a lush green valley in the mountains. What Uncle Willy told me that day in the barn gave me the strength and desire to survive the cruel and hurtful comments of my cousin.

"Claire, you wouldn't believe how amazing these horses are!" he told me. "They sound just like a train going by at a hundred miles an hour when they come galloping out of the mountains. Their manes blow behind them in flashes of black, silver, and gold like flying flags!" I listened to Uncle Willy's fantastic story, enthralled.

"Tell me more, Uncle Willy! Tell me more!" I pleaded.

"Oh, it's amazing, Claire, just amazing. You can even hear the different types of snorts and whinnies—they sound just like they're talking! Then all of a sudden in a gust of wind and dust they'll be gone. But…" He looked left and right, like he was about to tell me a secret, and then lowered his voice to a near whisper. "When they're gone, you're left with a feeling of magic. You know what it's like to be free and wild but still be a part of a family—a really *big* family!"

The images Uncle Willy conjured completely enchanted me, and I'd practically forgotten my cousin's spiteful words.

"I tell ya, girl," he added, "someday you have to go there. It'll change you forever."

I watched as he got a faraway look in his eyes and sighed as if he were there that very moment. I snuggled into the straw and closed my eyes, wishing I were there too.

"Someday," he promised me, "when you're older, you *can* go there. You'll see for yourself how beautiful those horses are. And here's the best part!" He smiled, and then said, "If you can catch a wild horse, it's yours! It will belong to you and only you for the rest of its life. That's the rule." Uncle Willy tousled my hair and pulled me upright with a grin. "Come on, now. Let's go inside and get some ice cream!"

I couldn't believe my ears. If what Uncle Willy said was true, and it had to be or he wouldn't have said it, I could actually have my own horse someday! I brushed all the straw off of my clothes and went back to the house with Uncle Willy for two big bowls of chocolate ice cream. But I couldn't pay attention to anything else he said. All I could think about were those wild horses.

As excited as I was about pursuing wild horses, in the weeks and months that followed, I knew better than to talk to anyone about my dreams. I had learned how quickly people will snuff out your dreams if you say them out loud. So I buried those words inside my Heart Horse, assuring him he would have company someday. He whinnied softly inside my heart, swaying back and forth as if to say, "We will wait, we will wait, we will wait."

Within every human being there are gods and goddesses in embryo with only one desire. They want to be born.
—Deepak Chopra

Chapter 1

Sweet Sixteen

When I turned sixteen, nothing happened. I thought girls had sweet sixteen parties, and everybody celebrated and felt happy. But nobody knew it was my birthday. Nobody ever knew. As far as I knew, I didn't really exist, because my birthday never happened. And if I didn't really exist, no one would notice if I disappeared.

And no one did.

I hadn't planned on leaving her that day. It was like any other day. I went to school; I came home; I did my homework and chores. After dinner I announced that I was going out with my friend Gail, and my mother tightened her face and told me I'd better be home early or else. Everything she said after that was just white noise. I tuned her out and took off.

I hadn't told her that we were meeting a couple of guys in their twenties and we were all going to get high. It's not like I was reckless or anything; I was an honor student and had already passed grade ten of the Royal Conservancy of Music, the highest level possible,

1

and I'd won several awards for my classical piano performances. She always made sure I could perform.

I liked hanging out with Gail. I didn't know her well, but she was very striking—a tall, thin girl with a pixie cut and great big eyes, heavy with mascara. She reminded me of Twiggy.

And like Twiggy, Gail wanted to be a model. She always did seem destined for something greater than Belleville. Our Canadian town on the northern shores of Lake Ontario was charming and quaint, but it was no place to plan a future. It was obvious Gail wasn't sticking around Belleville, which made her all the more intriguing.

I didn't know Gail's friends. They were older, in their early twenties. She was dating one of the guys, and the other guy was his friend. Smoking pot was what kids did back then, so that's what we did. It wasn't like we were getting in trouble. It was just a night out having fun.

As they were dropping me off in front of my house, I noticed my mother. She was standing in the sunroom, her hands on her hips, her neck stretched halfway across the yard, glaring as she tried to figure out who was in the car. I don't know what it was, but something about the look on her face that night, made me do it. I'd had enough.

One of the guys—not Gail's boyfriend but the other one—climbed out of the car to let me out, and that's when I did it. I knew she was watching. I had never kissed a guy before, but for some reason I reached right up, grabbed his head, and planted a huge, passionate kiss right on his lips. My mother was furious—I could tell by the throbbing anger flying through the air. As I walked past her and into the house, the jabbering began.

"You worthless whore! Carrying on like a piece of trash. We're Hitchons, you hear? Pillars of the community! We can't have you ruining our reputation with your antics. What will the neighbors think?"

"What will the neighbors think?" had become a familiar refrain. She may not have had much concern for me, but she had an awful lot of concern for the neighbors, and I felt an immense sense of satisfaction knowing that for once I'd actually given the neighbors something to think about.

But I knew she'd take it out on me. I knew whatever was coming was going to be bad, and I just didn't want to put up with it anymore. So while she was jabbering away behind me, calling me the spawn of Satan and that sort of thing, I picked up my guitar and my pink stuffed elephant—why I picked up my pink stuffed elephant, I have no idea, but that's what I did—and I walked out the front door as casually as if I were going to get the mail.

And I kept on walking, down the drive, past the mailbox, and down the street, while she screamed behind me, "What will the neighbors think?"

> Auntie Mame and Grandma are in the kitchen at the lake. Whispers pass between them as I listen at the door.
>
> "She fits in so well, don't you think, for an adopted child?" Auntie Mame says. "I'm so glad she is musical like her parents. Makes things easier to explain. I wish we could have been around more when she was little. I told you, Pearl, that daughter of yours was way too hard on her. We needed to watch out for her more." Grandma glances in the direction of the door and nods her head.
>
> I tiptoe out the side door and sprint to the lake like a deer fleeing a fire. I'm not sure what that all means. I'll find out someday; I know I will. That's my secret.

The police found me a couple of days later, but my mother didn't want me back. I was staying at my friend Brian Brown's place. Brian was my age, but he already had his own place in a rundown strip of row houses. They were pretty shabby, but that didn't matter. I just thought it was cool that he had his own place.

Since there weren't very many people our age with their own places, it wasn't very hard for the police to find me. A few phone calls was all it took, because, let's face it, there weren't many other places for me to go.

"She's pretty upset," my dad told me after picking me up at the police station. I could tell that he was upset as well, but I could also tell he was relieved to find me. My father was a big man with a small mustache, and he drove with both hands on the wheel, looking straight ahead. We drove in silence for what seemed like forever.

"I can't take you back there," he finally explained. "She isn't ready for you to come back." I knew she'd never be ready for me to come back. She wasn't ready for me to appear in her life in the first place. And now that I knew that, now that I had learned the truth about my appearance in her life, I knew I would never go back.

Mother tells me every day that she can send me back.

"Don't get too comfortable. If you don't do as I say, I'll send you back."

Back where? I wonder. *I thought I lived here.* But I really did wish she would send me somewhere else. That's my secret.

My dad rented me a room in a boarding house, and it worked out for a while. I was finally independent, but my dad stopped by and called regularly to be sure I was still going to school and staying out of trouble. Eventually, though, I had to leave when I got caught throwing a bag of pot out the window. I don't even remember why I threw a bag of pot out of the window, but I must have had a good reason at the time. Unfortunately, my dad was on his way over to visit me just when I tossed it, and it landed right in front of his feet.

To teach me a lesson, he called the police. They gave me a lecture, assured me I was on the path to ruin, said that if I didn't shape up, I'd amount to nothing, and then they sent me on my way. They didn't even ask about my mother; she was respectable, so why would they?

I got thrown out of the boarding house for tossing the pot, and still my mother didn't want me back any more than I wanted to go back. Her friend Mariel stepped in and said she'd take me.

Mariel and my mom had been friends for years; they were service wives together. My dad and Mariel's husband, Andy, always ended up getting transferred to the same places, so the two wives got to know each other pretty well. They were good friends, but once I moved in with Mariel, that pretty much ended their friendship. Mariel just had no idea what was really going on in that house—not until I moved in. Once she knew, I don't think she wanted to know my mother anymore.

> We had just taken our regular seats in church when the old lady sitting next to me leaned over, a dead squirrel swinging from her neck and breath like old feet, and whispered, "Oh, you look so pretty today, Claire. Your hair is always so nicely done, and your dress is so lovely." She didn't know that an hour earlier I was screaming in pain as Mother brushed my hair in a state of inexplicable rage and slapped me hard when I said I didn't want to wear

that dress. Nobody knows. Not now, but someday
they will. That's my secret.

I was living at Mariel's when I turned sweet sixteen, but as I've
said, no one really noticed. I didn't tell Mariel; after all, it was my
mother who should have thrown me a party. But, of course, the
only thing she ever threw regarding me was thrown *at* me, so I don't
know why I was expecting anything. I guess I was just hoping that
year would be different, since it was my sweet sixteen and all.

Then I got hit by a car and found myself in the hospital. My
mom blamed Mariel for not watching me better, and Mariel decided
it was best if I left. So that's exactly what I did.

Your pain is the breaking of the shell that encloses your understanding.
—*Kahlil Gibran*

Chapter 2

Psychedelic Nights

I found a new home with a group of other people living in a farmhouse not far from the city. One of the guys was Randy. Randy was a pot dealer who hung out with Brian and the gang, and I thought he was pretty cool, not like the guys in high school. I didn't even go to high school anymore, anyway, not since I'd run off to Brian's.

Randy was handsome and slender with long, curly dark hair and a mustache, and he dressed like a medieval poet, in puffy white sleeves and dark vests. In an era known for its fashion flamboyance, Randy always kept it understated, if not a touch theatrical.

Randy had a knack for theatrics. He entered every room as if he were suddenly on stage. But he kept his ego in check, while keeping us entertained. He had a great sense of humor, and he was full of energy. People were just naturally drawn to him. People always surrounded him, as if he was some sort of mischievous mystic. Like everyone who knew him, I always felt special when I was with Randy.

Randy took a liking to me almost from the very beginning. Most of the girls seemed to conform pretty quickly to their place in the counterculture, accepting their roles as pretty playmates and wholesome domestic queens. But a few of us didn't want to cook and sew and be content as dutiful co-wives. We wanted to be where it was happening, and that just happened to be among the men.

I didn't actually set out to be different; if anything, I think I was pretty naïve about the hemp selling, not realizing that in the sixties, women were expected to stay on the margins of the counterculture, not in its epicenter. I wanted to be in the epicenter. And hanging out with Randy seemed to be getting me there pretty quickly.

"Hey, babe," Randy said to me one day, putting his arms around my waist and talking into my neck and hair, shortly after we met up at Brian's. "I really dig how you're always doing your own thing, always close by, but playin' so hard to get."

I didn't see myself as playing hard to get at all. I simply wasn't ready for sex. After all, I was only sixteen years old and just barely out of junior high. This new world may have been opening itself up to me, but it was new, nonetheless. I was stepping into it cautiously like approaching a wild horse.

"Randy, stop!" I laughed, playfully peeling him off me. But before I could say anything more, his attention was turned away. It was someone asking him if they could score. Randy was the Pied Piper of pot; everywhere he went, a long line of pot-hungry hippies, looking to score, followed him.

Randy quickly noticed that while I wasn't at all promiscuous, I wasn't afraid to take some risks. The fact that I'd left home and run away, that I'd chucked my formal education for the chance to finally experience life and hang out with such hip guys, really seemed to turn him on. He just didn't quite know what to make of me; it was as if he'd never before met a girl who had her own thing going on, who played her own music and wasn't known as somebody's girlfriend. The combination of being risky but chaste really intrigued him. So it wasn't long before we were hanging out together pretty regularly.

"Come on, babe, I know you want me to be your first. Just a kiss, that's all," Randy said, taking my chin in his hand and looking into my eyes with his own dark, enchanting gaze. Never having had any experience with boys or men, except for that passionate kiss in front of my mom that sent me on my new journey, I was very innocent in many ways. Randy picked up on that. He used to tease me about how "sweet and sensitive" I was and yet how sad I always looked.

"You like to put on a tough front like you're some tough chick nobody'd better mess with, but I know you. You're my sad-eyed lady of the lowlands," he said, quoting the Dylan song that was popular at the time. "Why don't you tell me what you're so sad about, babe? You know Randy will make it better." He'd tease me like that in his gentle and fun way, but it was always in a sexual manner that made me nervous, scared, and most of all, happy to have so much of his attention when so many others were standing in line.

We often lay together on my bed, hugging and kissing, or sometimes Randy would just play with my long hair, gently pulling his fingers through it. It seemed an innocent enough gesture, quite gentle and loving. I don't think I was really thinking about what any of it would lead too. But I did know that Randy's persistence and patience had its limits, and it was only a matter of time before he would want to go all the way.

Since I had never really had any affection shown to me, to suddenly have such a cool and popular guy treating me like he really wanted and liked me brought me so much joy and confidence. And the fact that everyone who knew him liked him assured me I was with a good man. I also knew from the way we were going that eventually I'd give in to Randy, but until that time, I just wasn't ready to go all the way.

As he was slowly drawing me in, another thing happened. Randy and I were becoming a team. He was so charismatic and could convince anyone of anything that when he started talking to me about being his partner in the pot trade, instead of backing away, I felt even more special. After all, these were the sixties, and the pot trade was just an extension of the pot culture, with scoring a joint as common as scoring a Starbucks these days. No one ever really distinguished between smoking pot and selling it. If you had it, you shared it; if you didn't have it, you looked for whom ever did and compensated them for their costs and trouble. And Randy always had it. He didn't cheat anyone, and he had good stuff. It was only natural that people came to him to score, and his reputation as a reliable source quickly spread.

"I just can't keep up with everyone, babe" Randy said, "Everybody's looking to score, but there's only one of me to go around! But you and me together, babe, that'd be something. Wouldn't we make a groovy team?"

The images he'd conjure of us sitting back in Jamaica like the king and queen of the dope world, delegating and distributing while the music played on and the smoke swirled in the air, were to a newly runaway teenage girl in the 1960s; it was the next best thing to having a movie producer assure me he wanted me to be his leading lady. Randy was fast becoming counterculture royalty, and knowing he wanted me by his side when it happened was an incredible feeling.

One night Brian threw a party and I went with Randy. I remember I was on my period, and that was always inconvenient. My mother had never let me buy sanitary napkins. She made me use an old, ripped-up sheet folded into a pad. It was really uncomfortable and embarrassing. I hated gym class.

Since I was on my own now, I could buy Kotex, which was much better, even though you had to use this elastic thing with clips to hold the pad in place. I wasn't really in the mood to party, but this was a big party and everyone would be there. Not going was simply out of the question.

Brian's house was the typical drug house, always full of people smoking grass and high on various hallucinogenics. When we got there that night, the place was even more crowded than usual. It was packed with people, with candles and incense burning, Led Zeppelin on the stereo, and the smell of pot heavy in the air.

Brian's place had turned into a shambles since I'd left. The legless living room couch was sitting on the floor with plastic milk crates turned upside down for tables. Dishes were piled high in the sink, food was scattered all over the place, and clothes were piled in heaps wherever a mattress, closet, or sofa might be. I pretended I didn't notice the sour and rotting smells and how my feet stuck to the kitchen and bathroom floors. Instead I did my best to just be a part of the crowd.

It seemed like every room was infested with people drinking sweet Mateus rosé and passing enormous joints and getting high. Some people were really high, way beyond pot. They were floating around the house like they were having a dream, oblivious and amazed. Randy told me they were on LSD, and he said I should try some.

"Come on, babe," he said with his seductively persuasive charm, "you're going to love this stuff; it's going to blow your mind."

I hated the thought of not having control over my body, and I didn't want to try anything that strong. However, just about everyone there was doing it, and as always, Randy was persistent.

"Just a little one," he said, showing me a tiny pink pill that was so small it was hard to believe it could do anything at all.

"All right," I said, taking the pill. As much as I wanted to stay in control, I also wanted to know what all the fuss was about and why everyone was floating around so blissfully. So I swallowed the teeny pill, and before long I had completely forgotten I had done so, finding myself doing the party scene, joining one circle after another for a hit off a joint or a long suck on the hookah washed down with a swig of Mateus. But I didn't feel well that evening, and I couldn't quite get into the groove.

After a while I had to go to the bathroom. I hated having to use the bathroom at Brian's house, because it was so disgusting. What was once pink and green wallpaper was now so faded and shredded that long strips of yellowing wallpaper hung beside the toilet, which didn't have a proper seat. With no toilet seat on the toilet, I never dared venture in there unless I really had to go. Another feature, or lack of a feature, that made the experience so uncomfortable, was that there was no bathroom door. Instead of a door, they had nailed an old Indian bedspread across the doorframe.

When I sat down on the toilet rim, it was wet and freezing. I tried to squat over it, but my legs were wobbling so much that I couldn't do it. I lowered myself onto the cold toilet's edge and prayed that I wouldn't fall in. I could tell that others had made a pastime of peeling off the strips of wallpaper that hung from the bathroom walls. Strips of what used to be pink flowers hung around me as if I were in a paper garden—one that smelled of urine. I resisted the temptation to peel away the whole wall and relieved myself as fast as I could.

Just as I was zipping up my jeans, a huge form filled the doorframe behind the gauzy bedspread curtain. A big hand pulled back the dingy paisley fabric and long, straight black hair appeared. A head popped through the hair, and I saw a big grin on a dark and handsome face.

"Hey, don't worry, baby; stay if you want. Don't rush away," he said.

My cold fingers awkwardly struggled to zip up my jeans, but I hurried so fast that the zipper got stuck on my underwear.

"Here, let me help you," he said, smiling seductively. Before I could say no, his hand reached inside my jeans, and with the other hand he pulled the zipper down and then up. "See, no problem. Stick with me and it'll all be okay," he said as his eyes wandered slowly over my body.

The bathroom was no bigger than a shower stall, and as I stood in front of the toilet and he stood right in front of me, I could smell his breath and feel his body heat. I began to feel frightened and claustrophobic. I wanted to move past him, but his body was blocking the doorway and he made no attempt to step aside.

I tried stepping away from the toilet, but he leaned in closer and I could smell the sweet mix of aftershave and cannabis. His friendly smile and white teeth were nearly incandescent against his dark, honey-colored skin, and I felt a discomforting sense of attraction and anxiety.

I realized he must be an Indian. I'd never actually been close to a real Canadian Indian before. Even though there was a Mohawk Indian Reservation just on the outskirts of Belleville, we didn't cross paths much. Indians (which is what we called them back then) were almost a different species—exotic, sacred, and above all, dangerous.

My heart began racing as he moved in closer, until he was just an inch or so away. Part of me was frantic to escape, and my eyes were darting back and forth, looking for an opportunity to slip out of that uncomfortable scene. The other part was numb with questions and desires that a good girl would never think or feel, but I pushed those thoughts and desires out of my head and focused on getting away. I had to find Randy; then this guy would leave me alone.

"I have to go," I told him. Our faces were almost touching. He said nothing as his hands reached into my hair. As he brought me closer and his lips touched mine, his grip in my hair grew tighter.

"Get outta here," he whispered into my ear. "I'll catch up with ya later," he said with a sexy smile.

I pulled back the curtain and slid out of the opening, shaking and wondering what had just happened. I hurried down the hallway, trying to put some distance between my confusing feelings and me.

"Hey, babe. Where ya been?" A voice from around the corner startled me, and I saw Randy in the living room, surrounded by several people passing around a pipe. The strong smell of hash was so thick and pungent that I could hardly breathe. I watched in amazement as the swirls from the rising smoke made patterns in the air as if they are telling a story. The LSD was kicking in, and any doubt I had about that tiny pill packing any punch vanished as people turned into cartoon characters and words fluttered out of their mouths like dancing melodies. Forgetting all about the uncomfortable encounter in the bathroom, I began to laugh uncontrollably.

"What's so funny, babe?" A familiar voice appeared out of the smoke in letters, the twisting, lingering smoke spelling out each word the voice uttered. "Come on over and sit for a while," I read in the smoky letters.

I was laughing but at the same time feeling nervous and wondering who all these strange characters were and what were they doing at Brian's. It was as if my awareness had shifted from temporal and linear to spatial and present. I had no grasp of the past or future, only what was happening that precise moment.

My body felt spongy, and I could feel my legs shaking as the anxiety increased. *I shouldn't have done this,* I thought. *I want to get out of here and go home.* "Maybe I should just go and lay down for a while," I muttered to myself. "Yes, that's what I'll do."

I headed for the stairs, using the wall as a support. I felt like I was turning to liquid, and the house felt like it was moving and breathing, exhaling heavy sighs as I slowly made my way to the stairway and began the crawl upward. One by one, I lifted each foot, hoping there would be a floor to step onto and that the stairs wouldn't simply liquefy and dissolve. Meanwhile, the sounds from downstairs were turning into a foreign language I didn't understand. All I wanted was to lie down until it stopped.

After what seemed like an eternity, I stepped into cooler air and space. Cautiously, I slid one foot in front of the other, being careful to keep contact with the floor in case there were holes anywhere, as if I might step into a bottomless hole and be swallowed by the house at any moment. I felt the doorframe and slipped through it, and then I saw some sort of a mattress on the floor in front of me.

In one fast stumble I landed facedown on the damp, lumpy piece of foam. As I rolled over onto my back I wondered how many people had had sex on that foam and what they'd left behind. The room was spinning as I closed my eyes and smelled the musky odor of pungent sweat and old smoke. I just wanted it all to stop, the spinning, the hallucinations, and the weird sensations. I wanted it all to stop so I could go home. But I didn't really know where or what home was. I just knew it wasn't where I was. I just knew I didn't belong there.

The secret of joy is the mastery of pain.
—Anais Nin

Chapter 3

Love Hunger

"I'll be okay. I'll be okay. I'll be okay," I told myself. I could feel my eyelids fluttering like butterflies that had landed on my eyeballs. They wouldn't stay still. Then I heard a shuffling outside the room like someone dragging their feet.

"Hey, babe, you in there? You okay?" I tried moving my eyes to get the butterflies off, struggling to make out the approaching form, assuming it was Randy. Instead it was the Mohawk from the bathroom.

I tried to sit up but my body barely moved. Sweat had begun pouring down the sides of my forehead despite the room being icy cold. Everything in the room was moving—the walls, the bed, and the dresser, even the ceiling—and I could feel terror building inside me like vomit rising from my stomach.

The Indian crossed the room in slow motion and lowered himself on top of me.

"Shush," he whispered, the words falling into my ear like droplets of mud. "I missed you. I told you I'd catch up to you."

I started to say something, but he put his hand gently over my mouth.

"Shhhh... don't say anything. You're all right. I'm here now." The weight of his body pushed me into the lumpy foam, and I felt the hardness of the floor underneath, fearing that at any moment the floor could dissolve or swallow me up. The Indian's breath was wrapping me in hot steam. We were melting into one.

"Get off me, you prick!" I screamed, wondering if the words had even left my head. As I struggled to move, his grip got tighter and his hands slipped around mine, holding me tight. I was wedged between him and the floor, unable to move at all.

"Come on," he said firmly, his voice changing from seductive to increasingly assertive with every syllable. "Don't make this hard on yourself. Enjoy it. All the girls like me." The words don't make any sense in my mind. I wasn't sure what was happening, but I knew I had to get out.

"Daddy! I want my daddy!" I yelled into the empty air.

"Shut up! He won't hear you." She hissed as she sliced my backside with the long piano pointer. How could my daddy protect me? He never heard my screams. No one ever heard them. She sliced my back again. My pretty dresses would hide the wounds.

I felt Heart Horse begin to shiver. It had been so long since I'd felt Heart Horse—where had he been? He seemed to have disappeared ever since I left home, as if he'd stayed behind without me. But now he was back, nervous, wild, and nearly frantic. I wanted to calm Heart Horse, but at the same time, just feeling him tremble brought me courage. I wasn't alone.

"Have to get up. Have to go home. Move! Move!" I screamed at my body. I didn't know if I was screaming out loud or just in my head, but it didn't seem to matter. As Heart Horse began to run, the Indian's breath fell upon me like thick syrup, his breath the same rhythm as Heart Horse's gallop.

I knew if he tried to take off my clothes, I had a chance to get away. He would have to release his grip on my hands, and that would be my chance. I tried to concentrate on thinking clearly—which wasn't easy, considering his face kept turning into a kaleidoscope of monstrous creatures and demons and the house continued to pulsate with a life of its own. I waited for an opportunity to escape. Then, just as the Indian was getting ready to rip off my shirt, I heard someone coming up the stairs. He heard it, as well, and his eyes penetrated mine with a glare like a snake about to swallow its prey.

"Well, well, what have we here? So, you two having a party without me?" Thank God, it was Randy. He would stop it.

"Randy, help me! Help me! Get him off me!" I heard myself screaming as the Indian turned his head from me to Randy. But all I heard outside my head was muffled conversation. They were talking—talking while I was screaming.

"Help me!" I screamed at Randy, even louder than before. Didn't he realize what was happening? "Get the fuck off me!" I shouted, enraged as I tried once again to shove the Indian off me. This time I heard my own words. They weren't just in my head; they came out loud and clear.

"Oh, come on, babe," I heard Randy say. "This is the time. You have both of us now. No getting out of it."

Randy was at the end of the bed. His words sailed slowly through the air, smacking me in the face with the reality of what was happening. A scene I had only heard about was being played out; part horror story and part so unimaginable that I couldn't even say the words. I heard a high-pitched neigh from deep inside me and realized that Heart Horse was terrified. I could feel him turning in circles, growing smaller and smaller, as if to hide himself from the pending violence. Frightened as I was for myself and for Heart Horse, having him close by comforted me and propelled me to fight harder.

"No way! No way!" I screamed as loud as I could. I kept trying to push the Indian off of my body, but my desperate efforts barely made any impact, and he tightened his grip on me. Hot tears fell down my face, scalding my cheeks as he tore my white shirt, the buttons flying off, leaving trails like little comets in their path. Finally his hands released mine.

Now is my chance to get out, I thought. I pounded his back, but all I heard was laughter from the two men as Heart Horse rose up and kicked and kicked, making a furious racket. Randy was on the bed beside me, pulling my torn shirt off of me.

"You can't fight us, babe. Just let go," he said in a calm, loving voice.

"Get him off me!" I shouted at him. I tried to roll over and push the Indian off at the same time. With one quick swipe of someone's hand, my head snapped to the side, a stinging pain lingering on my cheek. When I opened my eyes, Randy was sitting on my stomach.

"You'll do as we say," he said, the loving tone gone. He leaned in close to my face, and in his right hand I saw a pocketknife throwing off sparks of iridescent light.

"See this?" Randy said, waving the blade in front of my eyes. "This guarantees you'll behave." As he moved it around, for a moment I thought it was a sparkler. The kind you get on fireworks days. Heart Horse knew better.

I felt the needle-sharp point of the knife scratch my cheek and saw a million red hearts erupt from my face and vanish into the air. "He's drawing a heart on my face," I silently told Heart Horse. "He doesn't want to hurt me."

"I do love you, you know," Randy said, smiling in anticipation of what he was about to do to me. The cold steel drew lines down my cheeks, wiping away the tears as it moved down my face and across my neck. "You'll do what I want now, won't you?"

The Indian had a hold of my jean leg hems as Randy straddled me, still holding the knife to my face. I tried kicking their bodies off of me, but my legs were pinned by their weight.

"I really thought you were cooler than this, babe," Randy said.

"Jesus Christ!" the Indian cursed, "Make her behave!"

I became a ragdoll, tossed from one to the other. Heart Horse had burrowed under my lungs where I could feel him with every breath. Every once in a while the knife would appear, and even through the hallucinogenic fog of my mind, I understood the threats. I felt another hot slap across my face, and my lip burst open, spurting blood all over the hands that previously held kindness. With a moan the room went black and I behaved.

> "If you don't behave and do exactly as I say, we'll send you back where you belong! Nobody will love you unless you behave." Mother always said this when she was mad. I do what she says, on the outside. On the inside, I feel different. That's a secret.

I had no sense of time. When it was over, I found myself alone, my face wet with tears. The foam mattress was cold and soggy with sweat and blood. Heart Horse was waking too, whimpering and licking me, comforting me with his love.

As I tried to sit up, my brain still wildly running amuck from the LSD, I slowly became aware that something horrible, something life changing had happened to me, but I wasn't quite sure what it was. I looked around the room and saw light beginning to sneak under the window blind. I wondered how long I'd been here. I looked down at my body, naked and bruised, dark blood smudged all over my legs. Had I been cut? I didn't know.

Confused, I looked for my clothes and carefully moved my body, which felt completely broken. As I struggled to get dressed, wincing in sharp pain with every movement, I wondered what horrors my body had endured and why I couldn't remember clearly. Every inch of skin was painful. I saw long scratches across my legs and chest that looked like writing lines, and bits of what had happened began to flicker across my memory and dissolve, practically as fast as they appeared. My lips felt swollen and blood was caked in the corners of my mouth.

"What happened, Heart Horse?" I whispered. Heart Horse whinnied softly in response, a gentle, sympathetic whinny that simultaneously assured and alarmed me. Something really awful had just happened to me. "I know I have to get out of here," I said to Heart Horse, in a barely audible whisper. "I have to get home somehow."

I gathered up my clothes and got dressed, wiping away the blood with a sheet that lay nearby in a twisted heap. As I crept down the stairs, I prayed no one would see me, that everyone would be gone. Looking down to the living room, I saw the air was thick with smoke. Candles had burned down to puddles of wax, and the record player had gone off its track and was making screeching sounds instead of music.

As I got downstairs, I glanced around the room. It was difficult to tell the bodies apart. They lay in a pile all intertwined, legs over legs and arms over chests. I didn't see Randy or the Indian anywhere.

Slowly, I made my way through, over, and across the passed-out people and into the cold early morning air. Each step sent piercing pain through me like a sharp bayonet. I clutched my shirt closed and walked as quickly as my body would allow, keeping to the back lanes so I wouldn't be seen. I felt the tears fall, knowing each one told a story of what had happened to me. The more I walked, the more the memories returned like flashes of terror that disappeared as instantly as they came. Somewhere between the breathing walls and cartoon faces of the night before and waking in the morning to the soggy foam bed, I had been violently attacked.

Yet at the same time, I knew that Heart Horse had returned in order to protect me, and that thought brought me so much comfort.

When I got home, I heard Randy snoring in his room. I went into the bathroom and stood in the shower, washing the wounds as gently as I could. As I watched the blood wash away, I fell apart in a broken pile of fears, thoughts, and tears for a night I would never forget, yet could barely remember. Then I got into my bed, and put the memory away in my Wall of Secrets.

I don't remember being really upset about it in the days and weeks that followed. Somehow I had learned to think of being abused as something that just happened in life, something impersonal and awful but momentary, to be forgotten.

I was really mad at Randy for a while. But he just seemed annoyed at me for being so upset. He said he didn't rape me, and that we just had sex. I didn't see it that way, but there was nothing I could do. I guess that's how our journey began.

*It is worse to stay where one does not belong at all
than to wander about lost for a while and looking for
the psychic and soulful kinship one requires.*
—Dr. Clairissa Pinkola Estes

Chapter 4

The Land of Oz

It wasn't long before Gail moved to Toronto, about two and a half hours west of Belleville, to start her modeling career. There was so much happening in Toronto. Randy went there all the time for business, and I knew the music scene there was really taking off. Joni Mitchell was a rising star on the Toronto coffee house scene, along with Neil Young and Gordon Lightfoot. It was the place to be. Anyone with musical talent went there; it was only a matter of time before they got discovered. And the art scene was inseparable from the music scene and just as exciting.

I was increasingly drawn to art, finding in my drawings and scribbling's a sense of peace and comfort, much like the calm I felt knowing Heart Horse was near. Heart Horse hadn't left me since the rape, but I felt his stirrings within me less and less as I settled into my new emancipated life. *If I can get to Toronto*, I thought, *I might be able to go to art school and become an artist.* "What do you think, Heart Horse?" I asked, but I could barely feel his reply.

Meanwhile, every day was another adventure, as our lives became a nonstop party that started soon after we woke up. People were constantly coming and going, and the smell of marijuana filled not just our home, but the streets, as ubiquitous as the rock and roll that blared from front porches, shops, and city parks all day and late into the night. These were colorful times.

"I can't keep up with all the demand here," Randy started muttering as long lines of customers lined up for a nickel or dime bag of his pot. "I'm spending so much time running back and forth between here and Toronto that I can barely manage my customers down here."

His business was thriving, and as with any small business that gets too big, he was considering expanding. It wasn't even like he set out with that goal in mind; the more popular he became as a purveyor of quality pot at a fair price, the more his competitors and suppliers started to notice. Opportunities for profit began raining from the sky as Randy considered how he could continue to supply his expanding customer base in Belleville and reach more customers in Toronto.

"You know, babe, you've got a knack for this yourself," Randy said to me one day. It was true I had developed a taste for pot and was making friends easily, but I hadn't given any thought to going into business like Randy had. "If you moved up to Toronto and started making some contacts, we could get a good thing going. What do you say, babe?"

I couldn't believe Randy would trust me so much to consider making me a business partner, and the idea of actually making some money and becoming as popular as Randy was exciting. But more than anything, I knew I just had to get out of Belleville. No matter what circles I was running in, it was still a small town, and I couldn't go anywhere without risking running into someone who knew my family. Going to Toronto was inevitable for almost any kid with ambition, and while I hadn't given too much thought to my future, I knew one thing: it was as far from my mother as possible. So I grabbed my guitar, stuck out my thumb, and headed for Toronto.

Heart Horse galloped in circles as a forest of concrete and steel appeared in the near distance looking like the Land of Oz awaiting us. But I wasn't expecting to find any wizards hiding behind any curtains. As excited as I was to reach Toronto, I was also a little bit scared. I figured that cities were the real wilderness, full of untamed and wild animals that would behave like hungry lions fighting to survive.

I knew, too, that those who weren't fighting to survive had finally given up. And some never thought to survive at all; those were the ones who wandered their way through life, oblivious to the savagery that surrounded them. I wished, sometimes, that I could live inside oblivion myself.

As I approached the city skyline, my body tensed and knotted, and I realized I was feeling carsick. By the time the grinding truck stopped at the side of the road, I wanted to vomit.

"Thanks, Ivan," I said to the trucker who had given me my last lift into the city. "Thanks a lot."

"Yer welcome, girly. Look after yerself," he said, his eyes scanning my cleavage one last time. With a loud slam, the truck door closed, shutting out the travelling odors of fuel, sweat, and cigarettes. The engines revved up, and with a wave Ivan was on his way, leaving me standing at the outskirts of Toronto, trying to find a pocket of air among the truck fumes and smog.

I adjusted my pack and began the walk to the city center. Each step felt like I was wearing concrete boots. Each breath sucked in dirt, grime, pain, and fear. In no time at all, my lungs were clogged with soot and microscopic debris; the wheezes and gurgles they made as I struggled to breathe reminded me that even taking a deep breath of the city air could be another source of danger. But I had survived my mother's wrath, and I was determined to survive without her. Still, I had no idea what would happen.

Just to avoid conversation with Ivan, I wrote in my journal on the drive to Toronto. I scribbled everything I had wanted to scream out loud for the last sixteen years of my life but didn't dare do for fear of her. I wore out two pencils just telling the story of my escape from her house. Once I reached Toronto, I closed my journal as if closing the past altogether. I would start a new life in my new city.

First, I had to find somewhere to stay. The air had the chill of autumn, and I realized that the city would be unforgiving in the winter. Already I missed my bed and my quilt that my Grandma had made. I had nothing like that with me—just a backpack with a couple of changes of clothes and a few toiletries. It would have to do.

Finally, streets appeared. Standing at Yorkville and Bay streets, I paused, looking in.

"This isn't going to be easy," I told Heart Horse. "But then nothing in my life ever has been!" I felt Heart Horse prance and nuzzle me, urging me on.

I saw a park nearby and headed toward it; it was the park Randy had told me about, where everyone hung out. This park would be my street home, I decided. It felt right almost immediately, and I knew I belonged, at least for the time being. Music in the background grew louder and the chattering voices of dozens of people were pounding in my ears. A Beatles song played from an opened window and I laughed out loud, though no one looked. "All the lonely people, where do they all come from? All the lonely people, where do they all belong?"

The newspapers called it the revolution, the love generation, the hippie culture. The labels made me smile. If people looked, I mean really looked, I thought, they would see it differently. They would see that it's the same culture as their own, only with more color and longer hair.

As the Beatles played on, and with a renewed sense of belonging, I shed my remaining memories of the past like an old skin and stepped into this new and magical world.

"Hey! Is that really you? S'bin a long time, doll." Jax wrapped me in a warm hug, tangling his twisted locks in my guitar strap. Jax was a friend of Randy's. I began to notice many familiar faces in the colorful crowds that surrounded me.

"Yeah, it's me. I'm finally here," I replied as I tried to untangle myself from his grip.

Several longhaired guys sidled up and we exchanged hellos. *At least here in the Village*, I thought, *we are all the same.* The people like my parents wouldn't dare venture inside these lines—too scared of all the weird-looking people, I figured.

I caught a glimpse of a guy I knew called Magic.

"Hey Magic," I yelled, waving my arms high over my head. "Over here. I'm here."

Magic saw me through the crowd and pushed his way toward me. With a huge smile, he wrapped me in an embrace, guitar and all.

"Hey! Put me down!" I laughed as he swung me around and then plunked me down on the grass.

I had just arrived in the city that would be my new home, and I knew I should have been jubilant, yet my body already felt weighted down with sadness and worry. Even the gruff old Ivan asked me why I was so sad. I should have felt thrilled, and I couldn't explain the empty place in my heart that seemed to haunt me the closer I came to my new life. There were so many pieces missing from my heart puzzle that I didn't know if I'd ever be able to find them all. But I knew that if I were going to survive, I would need some friends.

"Hey, Sunshine, whatcha want to do? Let's celebrate your homecoming," Magic said, bringing me out of my thoughts.

"Hmm, don't know. I'm awful tired after hitching up here," I said. But the conversation went no further. As if I had been there all along, Magic and Jax's conversation shifted, taking up where it left off before they'd noticed me standing there with my guitar. I listened to them talk about who was doing what and where, where to find free food, score drugs; it was just like Belleville in many respects, only busier. Magic rambled on about his latest drug high and what a kick it was.

I tried to chime in on their conversations, as if I had been there all along, but my words were lost in an air of hopelessness that surrounded the group that formed around us. I soon realized that everything they were talking about, everything they were doing, was all about survival. I decided not to mention my plan about helping Randy with his business. That could wait for another day. Survival is about right now and how to get through the night, and so that was what I focused on. As we stood there in the park, getting high and playing guitars, the evening covered us in a never-ending blanket of youthful desperation, and we snuggled together, trying to keep the cold away and the warmth between us.

As the days and nights passed and the winter set in, I learned to fall asleep wherever I found myself at the end of the day. I learned to make a soft bed of the cold earth in the city park, to find a warm corner in a dark alley or a dry sofa on a rainy night. I never slept in the same place twice, and I never worried about where I would sleep.

We were all vagabonds, a global family of runaways, and we would make room for each other.

I tied my guitar to my leg when I slept—just in case.

It wasn't long before I knew I couldn't keep sleeping outside much longer. The snow would be coming soon, and besides, it was hard living without a home—even for a hippie.

"I said its ten bucks a week. Didn't you hear me the first time?" As he spoke his eyes wandered up and down my body, sending chills up my spine. He was a landlord for a house on Madison Avenue I'd heard of where hippies could find a cheap place to crash if they didn't mind a crowd. He explained that it was an old Victorian mansion, converted into rooms, but before I could see it, I had to pay up front.

"I have to have the address first, and then you'll get your money," I told him. "You'll get it, don't worry. I'm honest."

"Yeah, sure you are. Just like all the rest of you hippies," he said. I didn't quite understand his contempt, considering we were his business.

"Please. I'll make sure everything is clean. I'll clean the bathroom and kitchen for nothing if you let me have it," I pleaded.

"Well," he conceded, his tone softening, "I guess that would be okay. Girls are better tenants anyway. Okay, the room is yours. But I'll be watching you!" With a smirk he handed me the key to the front door. I finally had a home—*my* home.

My first real home was a walk-in closet with a single mattress on the floor. The walls were purple and the ceiling and floor were black. There was about a foot of space along the side of mattress, but that was it. It was just enough room to put my guitar beside me, close like always but no longer attached.

My old house, her house, had twenty-two rooms; all filled with antiques and old people memories. Now I lived in a purple closet, but it was in a mansion. A giggle took hold, and I found myself laughing out loud at the absurdity of it all. In this house I shared one bathroom with ten or more people, each one of them pretty much like me. Some had bigger rooms but they cost more money. But I knew I had to start somewhere, so this would be the room where I'd launch the rest of my life.

"It will change, Heart Horse," I whispered, "once Randy and I are working together." Heart Horse whinnied softly.

I hadn't heard from Randy since I'd arrived. I'd sent some letters and tried calling, but he was always very busy. I wanted to tell him I was making contacts, but it could wait.

In my new home I met hundreds of people. The house was swarming with people, some sleeping in bedrooms, others bunking on every square inch of floor in what otherwise would have been a dining room, a pantry, a porch. I wandered through the house and realized I had already met some of the guys in the Village, but a few others I didn't know. I looked around the kitchen. Aside from being very dirty, everything seemed to work. I thought of all the fancy dinner parties my parents had thrown, and another chuckle burst out as I thought of how they wouldn't dream of setting foot in a place like this.

I went back to my room to try out the space and see how it felt. I stretched my body across the well-used mattress. It was lumpy, a nasty grey color, and had a musty odor. I tried not to think about who had slept there last.

Not bad, I thought, *this will work. I don't need more. I'm okay, I'm okay, I'm okay.*

The house was in a part of town that was at one time very wealthy. Most homes were large stately family boxes, similar to where I lived before. Tall maple trees lined both sides of the street. The houses were being converted into rooming houses, where the landlords took advantage of all the young people who were flooding the city. They rented out every possible space, whether a closet or an attic. Like mine, each room held a different story, and I wondered what the stories would be that my closet had to tell.

I spent the days wandering around the city, playing guitar in the Village, and meeting lots of interesting people. On really cold nights everyone would gather in the largest room in the house to share stories, music, and dope. I soon realized that the front room was the corporate headquarters for a few rising stars in the drug world, a place where every hippie in Toronto was bound to pass through at some point—and thus, an excellent place to hang out, score, and meet all the wrong people.

"It's enough for now," I told Heart Horse, "but not forever. I want something more for us." Heart Horse merely nodded.

What would life be if we had no courage to attempt anything?
—Vincent Van Gogh

Chapter 5

Losing Heart Horse

Some days, when the darkness of the city sky felt like a burden, I would sit alone in my closet, writing, thinking, and playing my guitar. In my heart and in my songs there was still an empty place.

"I'm still searching for the pieces to fill that hole," I wrote in my journal. "So far, I haven't come close. I don't think the missing pieces will be found here. My heart aches from such a thought."

I couldn't count the times friends told me that when they looked into my eyes they saw dark pools of sadness and pain. A friend even wrote me a poem about it. I hadn't been there long before I began wearing sunglasses, even indoors, to hide my lonesome eyes. I didn't want people to see my sadness. I didn't want them to feel sorry for me when I didn't even know the reason myself.

I wrote in my journal: "My closet door is open a crack and pungent wafts of smoke crawl through. I need some company to help me climb out of this despair. My nose follows the tantalizing smoke. It takes me right to the big front room, just like I thought it would. The door is wide open, and as I focus in the fog I see at least ten people lounging around passing pipes."

They had become my Yorkville family. One guy in particular became a good friend. His name was Dale. Dale was as skinny as a plucked chicken, with long, blond hair nearly to his waist. He loved to have me brush his hair. We'd chat like best friends, musing about our futures. Neither one of us thought we'd live to be thirty, but we did ponder where we'd be in another ten years—which seemed so very far away at the time.

Dale was very dramatic, and every encounter with him was entertaining. He loved the occult—he considered himself a practicing witch, with the power to manipulate fate. And one of our fates we were concerned with had to do with our landlord. Our landlord, Jack, was a nasty man who was constantly causing us grief over one thing or another. He was trying to squeeze more and more renters into the house, not repairing things, and hiking up the rent.

"Shall we put a curse on him?" Dale asked one day, completely serious.

"A curse?" I asked, laughing. "Sure, why not?"

"Claire, you mustn't laugh. The dark arts are very powerful. You must respect them."

I stifled my laughter and figured I might as well play along. I had been brought up in a Baptist Church, and after the minister tried to grope me, I really had no use for organized religion, though I was fascinated with Tibetan Buddhism and even went to classes. But Magic, especially dark magic and the occult, was something I wanted nothing to do with. Still, since I didn't really believe in any of it, I figured I'd humor Dale.

So we lit some candles. Dale set up a little altar and did some goofy ritual over it then began chanting to the spirits to punish Jack for being so nasty. I did my best to keep a straight face, because I could tell Dale took this stuff to heart. When it was over, he was laughing too, and we filled up a bong and got stoned.

A few days later, Jack fell down the stairs and broke his leg. I didn't laugh at Dale's dark arts after that.

The Madison house was like a perpetually changing commune of hippies, with someone leaving and a new person or couple arriving nearly every day. I wasn't there long before I found that hippies weren't the only ones who hung out there; every so often some bikers would come by to deliver weed or whatever, and they brought a completely different vibe to the house. I usually kept my distance when they came around, but one night, that just wasn't possible.

I stepped over legs and pushed aside bodies to get to my favorite corner—only there could I feel safe and ready to sit down. I had always liked having a corner to hide in, a place where I knew nobody could sneak up behind me. I wanted to see them coming.

Suddenly all eyes were on the doorway. A tall, well-built man stood at the door, flanked by a couple of grizzly bikers. There was something about this new visitor that changed the air. The temperature cooled, and the mellow atmosphere quickly evaporated. I assumed no one in the house knew him, and they were intimidated by the biker jackets, which I saw were emblazoned with "Satan's Choice" on the back.

"Hey, guys, what's new? Everybody cool in here?" the man said as he plowed through the bodies on the floor and collapsed in a grinning heap beside me. He was so close that my nose tickled with the smells emanating from him. *Cigarettes and beer with a sweat chaser*, I thought, *like a country western song that got stuck in my head.* I chuckled and moved a bit closer. He grinned.

There seemed to be something uncannily familiar about him that I couldn't quite put my finger on. I could tell he had a gentle spirit even though he pretended to be a tough guy riding with Satan's Choice. He molded into my side, leaving me nowhere to go since I was trapped in the safety of my corner. Heat passed through his jeaned leg into mine, setting off little sparks of concern. Normally I would have been happy to have the warmth of a friend next to me, but this kind of heat brought me a nervous chill. And the chill brought with it hundreds of tiny red flags—the kind I knew to pay attention to. I wanted to move away, but there was nowhere to go.

"My name's Kenny," he said, just like a boy scout. "What's yours?"

"Claire," I said as meekly as a girl scout. I couldn't conceal my nervousness.

"It's okay, Claire. I've seen you around. I won't hurt you. I just think you are pretty special. My guys think so too. You don't have to worry." The words slipped out of a lopsided grin, and his icy blue eyes twinkled with mischief. I stared at the two-day stubble on his face as he placed his left hand on my knee.

"Leave me alone, Kenny," I said, looking him straight in the eye. "I'm not interested. Get your hand off me."

"Sure you are," Kenny said, ignoring my plea. "After you see what I brought for you, you'll love me forever."

Heart Horse was galloping wildly, practically bouncing off of my chest wall. I knew he was warning me of danger. I tried to push myself up from the crowded corner. Already the warning prickles of heat were making their way upward. My face was flushed and sweaty.

Kenny grabbed my hand and pulled me down to the floor again on top of his knee.

"I said, let me go. Now let me get up," I told him, my irritation building. I wanted to leave, but his grip was like glue and I was stuck. I saw his arm was all covered in tattoos, monstrous animals and wild beasts with crazy eyes and sharp claws. I looked quickly around the room hoping to find somebody able to help me out, but nobody was paying attention to our little dance in the corner. *Shit. I'm doomed. Better not to fight him,* I thought. His grip tightened around my waist, and I relaxed into his body. He had won.

The rest of the group was huddled around the big-bellied biker Kenny brought with him; they didn't notice us at all. Kenny pulled me closer and whispered into my ear.

"I told you, you don't have to be afraid of the guys or me. I like you, *we* like you. We'll look out for you. That's Jeff over there. I've known him a long time. He's okay; you don't have to be scared of him. Relax, for Christ's sake." He grinned, showing his crooked teeth. "Now, if we didn't like you, that would be a different story, if you know what I mean," he said, as if half joking. I did know what he'd meant, and I didn't want to be a part of any different story.

Kenny reminded me of a mountain wolf, but not in a comforting way. My body tensed at the awareness of that thought. I wiggled myself around to face him and gave him the meanest look that I had in my expression bank.

"Okay. I'll sit here, but you better not touch me," I warned.

His grin spread from ear to ear, and he said, "Good girl. I promise I won't. Really. You can trust me." I doubted that, but it was enough to relax me.

I saw that his hand was inside his deep pockets, trying to pull something out.

"Hey. I want you to try something with me," he said, "It's special, just for you."

"I don't do drugs. Ever," I said. I wanted to tell him why, but I knew it was way too soon. He didn't need to know about the rape.

"Oh, come on. You'll really like this stuff. It was made just for you. It will take the pain away."

So he could see it, too? He'd only just met me, but the pain of the last sixteen years had scarred my face, and I couldn't possibly conceal it. If only it were true that there was something he could give me that would take that pain away, but I wasn't counting on it.

Looking around the smoky room, I saw several of my friends slumped over and a few were chatting like magpies. The atmosphere had changed. I wanted to run; only there was no place to go. Red flags were waving frantically from every nerve in my skin, and the chills caused a barely perceptible vibration that ran up and down me like an electrical current. I hugged myself and tried to brush my nerves into submission by rubbing my hands up and down my folded arms, but it didn't do anything to calm me and only made me more nervous.

I watched, mesmerized, as Kenny pulled out a little spoon with a bent-back handle. He set it before me as if it were an offering. With the same precision I used to organize my things in my closet room, he created a little place setting before me: spoon right here, piece of cotton there, glass of water at the top, and his lighter ready in his hand. Then he opened his other hand right under my nose. Inside was a plastic syringe.

"Shit no," I said. "No way am I doing that shit." Now I understood what was going on with others in the room, why everyone was huddled together in murmuring excitement.

I closed my eyes for a few seconds and debated, though I knew better than to consult Heart Horse. I knew it would upset him. Frantically, I searched my mind for signs of advice but found none.

Kenny squeezed my arm and pulled me close.

"It's okay. I'll be here," he said. "You won't be alone; I'll watch over you."

I hesitated. I knew I was about to do it, but I wasn't sure why. I knew I was about to change my life. Or was I? After all, I could always just do it one time, just to see what it was like. *There's no way I'll ever do it again once I've tried it*, I thought. I just wanted to try it.

"Well, okay," I told Kenny, "But just this once."

Kenny set about preparing the ritual. *He must have been a boy scout*, I thought. *Always ready, just like me. Maybe he's not so bad. Maybe it's just me. Maybe I'll be okay. Maybe.*

Ritual completed, syringe ready, Kenny expertly found my vein and injected a new world into the empty space that had been waiting. In an instant, I had a Street Horse cursing through my veins. But nothing about it felt right. It was all so very wrong. Where was Heart Horse?

My eyes were heavy, as was my heart. I slowly relaxed, and then just as I was about to nod off, a geyser of vomit shot its way up from my belly.

"Get out of my way!" I thought I was screaming but nobody moved. I jumped over legs and knocked over burning pipes and flew out the door to the bathroom down the hall. I folded myself over the porcelain bowl and peered down at the rust stains as drops of sweat splattered into the bowl along with my last meal. After several retching minutes, I was empty.

I fell back into the corner. The tile around me was gritty with the day's dirt. It was cold, and a layer of moisture had settled on top of the grit, leaving a sticky feel. I tried to wipe my forehead with my hand, but a layer of grit from the floor was imbedded into my flesh.

"Shit. What have I done?" I said as tears worked their way down my cheek.

My head snapped back to reality as I noticed jeaned legs beside me and heard the sounds of urine hitting water. It was Kenny. I couldn't believe he was peeing in front of me. He finished and sat on the toilet seat, looking at me.

"You okay?" he asked. "You sure left quick. I was worried about you."

"I don't know," I replied. "I had to throw up and then everything went black."

He grinned and handed me a dirty towel.

"Normal. Yup. It's normal kid. Don't worry. You'll be fine."

"You telling me this is fun?" I couldn't understand why anyone would have the desire to go through that a second time. If that's what it took to become addicted, I didn't have to worry. Kenny took the towel from my hands and began to wipe the sweaty grit from my face. His strong hands held my sagging shoulders.

His blue eyes looked through my brown ones straight into my soul as he said, "This will take all of that pain away. I know you have a lot. I just want to help. You gotta trust me. You'll be okay." He hooked his big hands under my armpits and pulled me upward, and I flopped around like a rag doll, letting him take control.

He supported me around the waist and gently guided me back to the front room and my corner. The room was much quieter. All I could hear was soft music with the occasional whispers of content.

Kenny lowered me back into the corner where he first found me and crowded in beside me.

"Just relax. Take some big breaths and it'll go away. Be calm, relax." He held my hand, and I let myself lean into him and put my head on his shoulder, breathing in his biker smells.

I'm okay. I'm okay. I'm okay. I'm safe. I'm safe. I'm safe.

A warm sensation slowly flowed into my body. My muscles relaxed and the nausea disappeared, taking with it my world of pain.

Heart Horse had come to a fast halt. He knew in an instant that Street Horse had replaced him. Kenny was right. Even the red flags had disappeared.

Must be a good sign. I'm safe, I'm safe, I'm safe.

For the first time in my life, I was free of pain.

You don't get to choose how you're going to die. Or when.
You can only decide how you're going to live. Now.
—Joan Baez

Chapter 6

Softly at Night

It's been a couple of weeks now that Kenny and I have been hanging out together. I've met all of the bikers living in the white house on Spadina Avenue. They all think it's cool having me around. Sometimes I cook for them and they laugh. To them I'm so young. To me I feel old. They promise to look after me and never let anyone hurt me again. And I've met the guy that sells the Street Horse. Kenny told me he doesn't like it. He likes to be all speeded up instead. That drives me crazy. Speed is bad.

Kenny always wore the same thing: black T-shirts, dirty jeans, and a thick leather belt with a biker symbol on the giant brass buckle. Although he had a leather jacket with Satan's Choice colors on it, he usually wore a denim jacket with pockets inside and out so that he could keep his stash and cash close to him. He wore dark glasses pretty much all the time, blocking out his magical blue eyes, but he would remove them just for me. And he chain-smoked

Export A's and smelled like old cigarettes, but at least he showered (unlike a lot of the guys), and his yellowed fingers were just a pale shade of yellow. He had a twisted arm, which made him very self-conscious; to compensate, he had covered it in tattoos of various animals so people would notice those and not his deformity. It must have worked, because that's what I first noticed about him when we met. Although he hated it, I loved his twisted arm. It was a small touch of vulnerability that set him apart from the rest of the guys. I was safe with Kenny.

I hadn't been at the Madison Avenue house long before it became clear that it was fast becoming one of the hubs of the Toronto drug culture. The vibe was dark and getting darker, and I knew I had to find another place to live.

"This place is getting a little too hot," Kenny said one day, "The Choice is renting another place over on Avenue Road. It's not going to be so busy; it'll be low key. And they're renting out the top floor. Why don't you move in there?" Kenny suggested.

"I don't know," I said, hesitating. "Those guys have been good to me, but everybody tells me if I hang out with them, I'll end up dead." The closer I'd gotten to the bikers, the more I found that underneath all that leather, they were really just ordinary guys. Some of them were even family men, with houses, wives, and kids in the suburbs. But they cultivated a pretty menacing image, so people who didn't really know them were naturally rather afraid. I wasn't afraid, but the more I hung out with Kenny's biker buddies, the more people warned me I was crazy.

"Come on, Claire," Kenny said. "You know these guys. They aren't going to hurt you; they're going to protect you. If you stay *here* much longer, you'll end up dead. These hippies here aren't watching your back; they're all out for themselves. If you move to Avenue Road, you'll have your own room and no one will mess with you.

Besides, the bikers will be on the ground floor; they're renting out all the rooms upstairs, so it won't be just bikers."

I sure did want a room of my own. And I wasn't afraid of the bikers. I'd heard all kinds of stories, but my own experiences with them had been nothing but good. Kenny was right; I was in more danger staying at the Madison house, where I'd have no one watching out for me, than moving to the Avenue Road house and having Satan's Choice watching over me. Besides, I figured given my choices between living with a houseful of bikers or going back to Belleville to live with my mother, I'd take the houseful of bikers any day.

It was a big white house with lots of rooms and hardwood floors. I didn't have any money, but since there were no other women living there, they said I could have a room if I did the cooking and kept the kitchen clean. I was pretty much doing that already at the Madison house, and all I got in exchange was a purple closet, so moving to the biker house seemed to be the only reasonable option.

There was a real bed in the room, and a dresser and table. There was even a closet, and no one slept inside it. The room was nothing special, but to me it was very special. I had space and I had privacy. And the guys couldn't have treated me better. I cleaned and fixed up the place and even hung a pair of yellow curtains in the window. They liked to tease me about my efforts to civilize the place, but I could tell they really appreciated it.

By cooking for the guys, I got to know them, and they appreciated the home cooking. They made an effort to show up for my dinners, and sometimes, like when I made a special dinner or something, the word would spread that Claire was cooking a chicken dinner, and sure enough, we'd have a houseful.

Kenny was right. They weren't about to hurt me, and they certainly could protect me. No one messed with me once they realized where I lived, and it wasn't long before I was able to safely start dealing a bit of heroin myself, in order to keep my Street Horse fed. I knew enough people that I had a steady stream of customers, and the bikers were able to keep me supplied and protected.

In return for the room, I kept the place looking nice, cooked dinners, and washed the dishes. As for the non-bikers renting rooms upstairs, that just never happened. Bikers took over the whole top floor as well as the lower, but that was fine with me, just as long as they didn't mind me having some of my hippie friends over every once in a while, and they didn't. I wasn't there long I before felt safer than I'd ever felt in my whole life, and I was accepted into the group like their kid sister. It was the closest I'd come to having a real family.

> Another family reunion. Another day filled with cousins talking about us. The three of us were huddled together under the apple tree near the creek. Everyone else was laughing and playing catch, running around chasing each other. We were not invited to play. We were the adopted ones, my two cousins and I. We were to be kept separate, a different tribe and not part of "the family."
>
> *Someday I'll have a family* I, thought, *someday, but not now.* That's my secret.

One of the hippie friends I still hung out with was Dale. After all, who couldn't use a friend with magical powers? Ever since he put the curse on our landlord who then broke his leg, I was a little freaked out by Dale. But in a good way; he was certainly entertaining! Like me, Dale had also developed a taste for heroin,

43

and one night he came by shortly after I'd scored a new bag of junk to help me cap it in gelatin caps to ready for sale.

Naturally, as we filled the caps we enjoyed lots of samples, and before long we were nodding off, occasionally scratching our noses, our eyes slits of drug-induced semi-consciousness. It was extremely powerful stuff, some of the best I'd had, and the more we did, the deeper we slid into oblivion. After we'd capped it all, we lay on the bed talking, laughing, and listening to music until we both fell asleep, snuggling together on the single bed.

Early the next morning I got up, as I always did, long before anyone else. I whispered a good morning to Dale and told him I was going downstairs to get some coffee, but he didn't respond. I reached over and gave him a shake, but still nothing. Then I took a good look at him and saw that his face was blue; his arm was hanging over the edge of the bed like a pendulum, with a needle stuck in his vein. There were a few dried blood spots on the floor right below his hanging arm.

I jumped out of bed and started screaming for help. BJ and Sparky came running upstairs. BJ was a really tall guy with a long, thinning ponytail tied back with a leather lace. His hands were huge, and his arms were covered in tattoos of knives, swords, guns, and girls. The tattoos were a swirl of blacks, blues, and grays with little red tattooed drops of blood representing, he said, the guys he'd killed.

BJ and Sparky had been up all night long talking something over in the kitchen, and he sure looked like he'd pulled an all-nighter. BJ was dressed in greasy blue jeans and a gray T-shirt underneath his black leather biker vest. His face was bright red with the speed flush of a recent hit, and his neck was covered with a lacework of blue-green veins pulsing through his flesh from what must have been a skyrocketing blood pressure. He looked like he might explode.

I didn't have to say a word; I just stood there, looking down at Dale lying motionless. Standing so close to BJ, I could smell stale cigarettes, beer and that pungent stink of sweat-laced speed leaking from his pores. He leaned over Dale, his long greasy ponytail swinging like a spike, and tried to revive him. He shook him, yelled at him, and rolled him over, but Dale wouldn't wake up. When BJ stood back up, I noticed the huge tattoo on Dale's back. It was of angel wings.

"Call an ambulance," he barked. His voice was as gruff as he looked; there was nothing the least bit sentimental about BJ. He and Sparky went back downstairs to wait for the ambulance, and I quietly followed, feeling stunned and shocked into silence.

"Don't worry about it," Sparky said to me as he opened another beer. "Happens all the time. The cops won't even come here." After taking a swig of his beer, he set it down, lit up a joint, and passed it to me.

Sparky was old enough to be my father. He had a big, round belly and a deep, melodious voice. His stringy salt-and-pepper hair hung down to his shoulders, crowned with his biker cap—probably to conceal a thinning hairline—and he wore dark glasses, even inside. And just like BJ, his jeans were so dirty that they were practically growing new life forms. I don't think any of those guys ever washed their jeans. They wore them until they disintegrated and then bought new ones.

But what was most memorable about Sparky was his arm. One of his arms was rippled with waves of scars in a pattern that looked like a crumpled piece of paper that had been flattened back into shape. Rumor was that he had been in a fire at a drug lab and was lucky to be alive.

That arm fascinated me. Some of the ridges were white and some were brown, giving it the appearance of snakeskin. When I was high, the arm looked just like a snake, and sometimes I would find myself staring at it, trying to see faces and animals in the designs of his scars. Sparky would roar with laughter at my fascination with his arm, and he liked to tease me with it by pretending it actually was a snake reaching toward me.

But as much as his arm fascinated me, his yellow-stained fingers repulsed me. They smelled like cigarettes, and I tried not to breathe as he reached out and gently pushed my hair behind my ears. Then ever so gently, Sparky's snake arm untied his black neck scarf and handed it to me to wipe away my tears.

"Thank you," I said softly, smiling at Sparky through my tears.

The whistle of the teakettle suddenly pierced the silence with its shrill scream, and I made cups of Nescafe instant coffee for the three of us. We sat in the kitchen, watching the morning light filter in through the yellow curtains that I had hung not so long ago but what felt like another lifetime.

The minute the ambulance arrived, chaos erupted. The EMTs pulled Dale off the bed, and he just slid like a snake, as if he didn't have any bones. It was evident to them he was dead. They didn't ask what happened; they just took him away. One with a clipboard asked me his name.

"Dale," I said, still shaking.

"Last name?"

I didn't even know his last name.

In individuals, insanity is rare; but in groups,
parties, nations and epochs, it is the rule.
—Friedrich Nietzsche

Chapter 7

Silence Is Golden

I don't remember when I first noticed that Kenny was starting to change. He was clean-shaven with short hair when we first met, but it wasn't long before a bald spot appeared on the top of his head. It was nothing at first, just a small spot where his hair thinned enough to let his scalp show through. However, the hair got thinner and thinner, and the spot got bigger and bigger until it was unmistakable; Kenny was going bald. And the more hair he lost on the top of his head, the longer he let what was left of it grow—and the more hair he grew on his face. After several months, his thinning hair was down to his waist, and he had grown a long, wild beard that was speckled with gray bristly hairs that poked my face when we kissed.

Kenny came by pretty regularly, and occasionally he stayed over. We weren't exactly living together, but I let him stash a bunch of his things under my bed. He was always coming and going and had a pretty busy life. He just wasn't the kind of guy you would expect to be fixed in one place. He spent a lot of time going back and forth to Kingston on business, and every once in a while he would even disappear altogether. That's just the way he was.

One afternoon I was tidying up my room and started to sweep under the bed. I pulled out the boxes he'd stashed under there in order to sweep it clean, when my curiosity got the best of me and I took a look inside one of the long boxes. It was filled with guns, ammo, and hand grenades. Hand grenades. I couldn't believe it. I had been sleeping on top of hand grenades for how long? When Kenny finally got back, I really let him have it. I raised hell and told him I wanted those hand grenades out.

He got rid of the grenades but acted like I was hysterical or something, getting worked up over nothing. We never talked about it again. I didn't care about the guns. He needed those, he said, for business.

It was true he needed the guns. With the transition from smoking the peace pipe to shooting speed, things started happening very quickly. What had started out to be just a bunch of pot-smoking hippies listening to folk music in the park had turned into a high-stakes battleground of drug dealers dead set on conquering territory. And I hadn't been with them long before I realized that the guys in Satan's Choice were in the maelstrom of the battles.

Satan's Choice was the biggest biker group in Ontario, with branches in all the cities. But they weren't the only one. A local group, Para-Dice Riders, was trying to move up the biker chain and expand beyond Toronto. Unfortunately, their smaller size didn't make Para-Dice any less significant; instead, it made them all the more aggressive. They wanted to expand their territory rapidly and to do that meant going after our territory and our customers. Once they set out to do that, the biker wars began.

I was kept far away from the front lines of the war, but I had a ringside seat to the weirdness and the bloodbaths. One of the worst problems was the speed. Kenny thought speed was the perfect high—it kept him busy and making money, and he thrived on the adrenalin rush. But I didn't like it at all. I didn't like the frenzied high, and I didn't like the way it changed people. I could already see it changing Kenny. It was getting so I couldn't tell when he was being cautious and when he was just plain paranoid, but more and more often he was glancing out windows, recounting his money, and glaring at this guy or that guy he was convinced wasn't being straight with him.

It seemed that the more popular speed became, the more paranoid everyone was becoming. We all began living in fear, but the speed freaks lived in their own world of suspicion. Guys like Murray the Speed Freak ran around with bloody noses and twitching limbs, their heads swiveling back and forth in hypervigilance for anyone out to get them. I'd see them wandering around in the middle of the night, picking up little pieces of tinfoil or scraps of paper, gazing at them like they had found something inexplicably strange or hopefully a piece of hash or a tiny granule of speed. They'd even hide behind garbage cans, thinking anyone sitting in a parked car was obviously a cop.

The truth was the cops weren't much of a problem at that point. They were too scared of the biker gangs to do much damage, but just the fact that they could, and sometimes did, arrest someone, heightened the paranoia. But it wasn't the law that was the real threat; it was the outlaws. They were good to me, but that didn't mean they were good to each other. If they weren't ripping each other off, they were assuming they'd been ripped off. It got so that practically every drug deal was accompanied by someone accusing someone else of ripping them off, being a narc, or just plain disrespecting them.

As protected as I was, however, it turned out I was a lot less safe than I'd presumed. I hadn't realized that I was actually more vulnerable. By going after me, Para-Dice Riders could control the people who cared about me.

Although I kept to the sidelines for most of the deals, I used to go out with Kenny on some of his drug deals, to act as a distraction and even a deterrent from violence. I wasn't used to violence, fights, or guns, but once I found myself living with the bikers, I quickly adapted. Guns and violence were just sort of taken in stride, part of the lifestyle we were living. You couldn't succeed in the drug business if you backed down easily; you had to be tough and let people know you were tough. It was quite a contrast from the flower-child atmosphere I'd first stumbled into, but it was an exciting environment where I was valued and respected and my friends let me know I belonged.

I hadn't ever had those feelings growing up, and to experience them for the first time, while medicated with Street Horse into a state of perfect nightly bliss, was something I wasn't about to give up lightly. For the first time in my life, people cared about me. And for all his faults, I knew Kenny cared about me in a way that no one, not even Randy, ever had.

I finally realized just how out of control everything was becoming when one of Kenny's drug deals went weird. It was a huge deal with the Para-Dice guys, and we knew that working with another biker group could be very unpredictable. This one was wrong right from the start. Nothing was organized, phone calls were late, and people weren't showing up at the right times. It was all going wrong, and Kenny was on edge. I was nervous as well. I knew guns were involved, and that didn't bode well, but Kenny had to be protected.

What I had heard about the Para-Dice Riders wasn't good. They were easily set off and tended toward violence. Now that drugs and money were involved, the chance of a smooth and profitable deal seemed remote. But they were looking to buy some drugs, and

Kenny was looking to sell some drugs, and the profit margin was huge. It wasn't a deal he'd walk away from, that much I knew.

After several phone calls and changes to where we would meet, they finally settled on an address.

"I'm not worried about any trouble," Kenny said as he loaded his gun. "I know these guys and they're cool. They won't hassle me, especially if you're with me. Don't worry." He shoved the gun in his waistband.

"I don't know, Kenny. Are you sure this whole thing is a good idea?" I asked him. "Why don't you just play it safe and forget it?"

Kenny glared at me, and I immediately regretted saying anything. I knew there was no playing it safe in this new world.

It had become the standard practice to check out the scene before bringing any drugs to the buyers. We knew if we just showed up with the drugs, the chances of being ripped off were huge. It made more sense to show up, check out the scene, have a conversation, and be sure the money was there. If everything looked good, then I'd hang around with the buyers while Kenny went back for the drugs. That was the plan.

We drove for quite a while, stopping several times for Kenny to make some calls, until we ended up in suburbia. I was lost out there; I'd never been to that area before, and if anything went wrong, I'd have no idea how to get home. Even walking up to the door, my legs shook. I had a bad feeling in the pit of my stomach, and nothing Kenny said could calm me.

The minute the door opened, all hell broke loose. I stepped into the front hall, and in a split second a pair of strong hands grabbed me from behind and pulled me into another room. There was so much yelling and chaos that I didn't know what was happening, and then suddenly, all was quiet.

I knew not to open my mouth. I knew if I said anything, the grip would only tighten. I heard a door slam and Kenny cursing on the other side, yelling that if they hurt me he would fucking kill them and war would be on.

I was yanked and dragged through a roomful of bikers all riled up and waving sawed off shotguns in my direction. The stench was overpowering. The smells of sweat, beer, drugs, smoke, and testosterone were magnified ten times over. I was careful not to look at anyone as I was pulled through the kitchen, down rickety stairs, and out the back door toward a waiting car.

"Get in and keep your mouth shut," a huge, muscular biker ordered as he pushed me into the back seat and climbed in beside me, gripping my arm tightly. "Go!" he yelled at the driver. I thought the driver must have been trying to earn his patch because he looked as frightened as I felt. He kept glancing at me in the mirror with a nervous twitch in his startling blue eyes, and I knew it might be the last car ride I'd ever take.

So, it's all gone bad, I thought. *They're going to rip Kenny off for the drugs. He's probably gone to get them, and they'll exchange me for the bag—or kill me.*

We rode for what seemed an eternity while the big guy continued to hold me tight. I could feel the heat from his body; it felt like I was being burnt. His grip would relax for a second and then tighten until it felt like my arm would fall off from being numb. I stared straight ahead, not saying a word. I was sure he could see my heart pulsating through my top, and I could feel his eyes drilling holes in my body as he looked me up and down. We were both sweating, but for different reasons.

We eventually turned down a long dirt drive, and the car slowed to a stop. Muscle man and another guy picked me up and carried me up the stairs into the back kitchen where I was plunked into a chair like a sack of potatoes. Then someone yanked my arms behind the back of the chair and tied my wrists together. I tried not to look around, but I was mesmerized by at least ten pairs of eyes staring at me. Half a dozen sawed-off shotguns of various sizes were pointing in my direction. Muscle man was beside me with a gun at his side. Every few minutes he would point it at my head and adjust his position and then let it fall back to his side.

"Here's what's gonna happen," a tall, bearded biker with cold grey eyes said like he was discussing vacation plans. "We'll give ya back if your man brings the dope. If not, then we'll have some fun."

I looked around at the grinning faces. All were sweaty with the odor of stale testosterone oozing out of their skin—man smells.

"Yup. We'll just have to wait and see," he said as he brushed the gun barrel across my chest. I said nothing. Silence was best in that kind of situation. I felt Heart Horse shiver.

I really had to pee. I was tied to the chair, and my arms hurt from being pulled behind me and tied for so long. I didn't know if they'd shoot me or rape me, but the one thing I couldn't get off my mind was that I had to pee.

I looked around the room, but all I saw were men. There didn't appear to be any women around. Maybe if there had been, I would have felt safer asking them if I could go pee. The situation was bad enough as it was. No sense giving them even more power over me by asking them for anything, even if it was just a toilet and some privacy. So I kept my mouth shut.

Other than the muffled conversations going on around me, the house was silent. We were waiting.

They took turns walking around the table, touching me as they passed—touching my hair, my cheek, and my lips, touching my soul. I wanted to spit at each one as they passed, but I kept silent and emotionless. Muscleman didn't move from his post. I could feel his eyes still boring holes through my clothes. It was almost as if he were waiting for me to look him in the eyes and acknowledge his attention. I didn't.

The sun had gone down and lights were turned on. That meant I had been sitting there for most of the day. I knew Kenny would come. Of course he would. I wondered what was taking so long and what would happen when he showed up. But most of all, I wondered when I'd finally get to pee.

I was numb from sitting and my arm felt frozen and tingly. I didn't want to ask them for anything, but I couldn't endure it much longer. Then, just as I was thinking of asking if they could change my position, the muffled conversations burst into angry yelling. Muscleman thrust the gun at my head, and the room was suddenly swirling with bikers and guns. I couldn't tell who was who or what was going on. It was just a sea of jackets and guns swirling, swearing, and shouting all around me. Whatever was going to happen, it was starting to happen.

"Where is she? I want to see her!" Hearing Kenny's voice was an incredible relief; at last he was back. Seconds later his face appeared in the doorway surrounded by a cluster of mean and ugly biker faces who glared at Kenny with such contempt that it seemed more probable they'd kill him along with me than let me go with him.

"First you give us the drugs," Muscleman ordered, holding his gun at my head.

Kenny reached into his jacket and pulled out a big plastic bag filled with white powder. He handed it to one of the bikers who opened it, stuck his fat and dirty finger into his mouth, and then plunged it into the bag and back into his mouth for a taste. He grunted an acknowledgement that it was, indeed, good shit.

"Now let her go!" Kenny demanded, but Muscleman just sneered.

"Not so fast. We haven't decided what to do with her yet." Muscleman stroked my face with the tip of his gun then moved it slowly down my neck and across my chest, poking into my cleavage.

I was wearing a burgundy-colored flowered blouse with a yoked collar and puffy sleeves. It was one of those heavy cotton peasant blouses that were popular at the time, cut loosely like a smock.

"Leave her alone! She's pregnant," Kenny lied.

Muscleman glared. "Pregnant?"

"Yeah," Kenny said. "Almost five months."

Almost five months? *Thanks, Kenny*, I thought.

Muscleman pulled his gun away and snorted, "That true?"

"Yeah," I lied. "Fourteen weeks."

"Look, you got the shit, now let her go."

There was more murmuring behind my head—angry voices, drunken, stupid voices.

Then suddenly someone said, "Untie her! Untie her!" I didn't know who was yelling, but in one swift move I was taken out of the house as fast as I had come in. This time I was pushed into a car and told to lie down on the floor. Then Kenny and BJ magically appeared, climbing into the front seat, and we were gone.

I felt like vomiting. I couldn't stop shaking and was too terrified to say anything, much less get off the floor of the car. We rode over the bumpy dirt drive and onto the dark streets in silence. When we were safely miles away, I felt the car stop, and Kenny opened the door. I cautiously rose, and then I fell out of the car, vomiting into the black night. Kenny was right behind me and wrapped me in a blanket. When I turned toward him, I saw he was grinning from sparkling blue eye to sparkling blue eye.

"Well, that didn't go so well, did it?" he asked then he hugged me to his chest, and I clung to him, shivering.

Then, when I knew I was really, truly safe, I finally said it.

"Man, I need to pee."

Memory is the diary we all carry about with us.
—Oscar Wilde

Chapter 8

Somebody Help, Please

When I'm alone I don't think about Kenny. Or Randy. I think about my mother. I think a lot about the things she did to me. If I close my eyes, movies play out in the darkness of my mind, bringing the past to life behind my eyelids. I should feel the pain of those secrets, but I don't, not now. Street Horse keeps them away. I know I'll think about them later when Street Horse dies.

After I was kidnapped, I started to realize what a dangerous world I was living in. Kenny still needed to come up with the money to pay for the drugs he'd swapped for my life, so there was some ongoing tension with Satan's Choice. And people were starting to drop dead with regularity; even Maury the Speed Freak, otherwise believed to be invincible, had overdosed. One day a body was tossed on the lawn, just thrown there like the morning paper. No one ever explained that one to me, but they seemed to know what it was about, and I had sense enough not to ask.

But as bad as things got, I really had no idea how to make my life any safer. I needed to keep dealing myself in order to feed Street Horse, and Kenny needed to keep his business going. It was clear that it was only a matter of time before something really bad happened. We didn't talk about it all that much, but one day Kenny said it wasn't safe for me to live there anymore.

"We need to split from this scene; it's getting too crazy. I don't know half the people anymore, and it's got a bad vibe. We need to get our own place, a safe house no one can find."

Our own place. I loved the idea of a home of our own—a place I could fix up and cook dinner and know Kenny and would come home at the end of the day. Somehow it didn't seem the least incongruent with our actual lives, which were filled with people coming and going constantly, often until dawn. I was just so happy to think that we could get out of that madhouse and into a home of our own.

It didn't take us long to find just the right place. It was a conventional-looking brownstone duplex a few blocks away on a tree-lined street where kids rode their bikes and people tended their gardens. There was an alleyway between our house and the one next door that led to a discreet side door opening to the basement rooms that we rented.

It was cold and dark, but it was our own place, and it was very private. It was a basement studio apartment—pretty much just one large room with a kitchen running along one wall and a tiny bathroom not much bigger than a phone booth. That was it. A row of windows on the front side overlooked the yard; the grass was at eye level, which made it difficult for anyone to peer inside the windows without getting down on their hands and knees. The minute we saw it, we knew it was just what we needed. We wanted a place where we could come home to peace and quiet and Kenny could stash some drugs. After all, that was his business. I didn't care. I had my Street Horse, and he kept me busy. I had to feed my Street Horse. Kenny had been right; Street Horse took the pain away.

We moved into our little house, and I tried to make it into a cozy and safe home. I was burned out from the constant parade of people at the Madison house and just didn't have the energy or strength to keep partying every night. Most times I just wanted to crawl into bed and stay there. Our home would be our refuge from the insanity and a new beginning.

I got to work on it right away. I scrubbed and disinfected every square inch, washing away years and layers of grease, grime, dust, and mold. The bathroom and the refrigerator were caked in black mold, and I scrubbed them until they were sparkling. But no matter how clean I got the place, I couldn't get rid of the cockroaches or rats that I soon discovered had made a refuge of our cool, dark apartment. I had never before seen either a cockroach or a rat since living in Toronto, but now I was living side by side with them both. But once again, I learned to adapt.

We furnished the apartment with a mattress on the floor, which I kept made up with proper sheets and pillows so that it felt as clean as possible. Even though it was carpeted, there was no padding beneath the carpet, so the floor stayed cold and hard. We found an easy chair with no legs and covered it in a blanket and added a plain wooden coffee table, some plastic milk cartons for our record albums, and a few big cushions on the floor. An old arborite kitchen table and chairs, a few books on the windowsills, and a couple of posters on the paneled walls, and it felt absolutely perfect.

The neighborhood was noisy and colorful, with children playing outside and families arguing or laughing from their front porches. The neighbors were mostly Italian or Portuguese immigrants, and we could always smell something delicious cooking. But I didn't have much appetite for eating. I didn't have much energy and was losing my appetite completely.

"You're getting skinny, girl," Kenny said, wrapping his muscular arms around me and pulling me close for a kiss. "We need to fatten you up! And your eyes are all yellow. What's that about?"

His words stung, even though he was just being playful. Kenny had started making comments about my weight more often, and the recurring reminder that I wasn't up to his standards of beauty only brought me down. I didn't think I was skinny. I didn't feel skinny. I felt not fat. But I *was* losing weight; there was no doubt about that. Curling up on my side I would try to find a comfortable place on the lumpy mattress to read, smoke, or sleep, and I'd feel my hipbone hit the cold, hard floor underneath. I ran my hand down the side of my torso and let my fingers play over the hills of my ribs.

Maybe he's right, I thought, *I have lost a lot of weight.* But I didn't do anything about it.

As comfortable as our secret home was fast becoming, life outside the house kept getting in the way. Days melted into weeks, weeks into months. Time didn't matter anymore; only Street Horse and Kenny mattered. I ran into Randy every once in a while—he had moved to Toronto shortly after I had—but his world had become another lifetime. Now I was living in Kenny's world, and what a world it was.

I didn't make it back to the Village for a while. The desire to sit and play music with my new friends, my plans to go to art school, just like the plans to go into business with Randy, all got lost somewhere between Madison Avenue and our new secret home. I didn't care. I had a home. I had someone who cared about me. I had Street Horse. I didn't feel the pain anymore.

The whole idea about renting the house was to keep it a secret. Kenny made me swear not to tell anybody about where we lived, and he said he wasn't about to tell anyone either. A house we could retreat to at the end of the day was not just a personal refuge, it was an insurance plan. Kenny needed a place where no one could find him—no one but me—in the event anything bad went down. It made a lot of sense.

So when I came home one night to find the house filled with people—people I didn't know—I knew something terribly wrong was going down. Our secret home was no longer a secret, and that meant it was no longer safe.

I didn't say anything at first. I walked in, Kenny acted like everything was normal, and I just sort of buried my shock and anger and joined the party. After a few hours they all left, except for one guy who was sitting on the floor beside the mattress. He and Kenny had been talking business all day. I didn't care. I just wanted him out. I was tired. I had no energy for playing hostess. I just wanted our happy home back.

I must have fallen asleep. When I woke up the room was dark and quiet, the air heavy with the stench of sweat, skin, and drugs. *Air. I need air,* I thought.

My chest felt terribly tight, and I couldn't get any air into my lungs. It was a struggle to sit up and an even greater struggle to breathe. I had to return to reality, but my mind was far behind. We must have been doing drugs for hours. My body just wouldn't work right. I had to get up. I had to get air. I rolled over and off of the mattress, and my feet hit a warm lump. I tried to push it out of the way with my feet, but it wouldn't budge. I didn't even think to ask who or what it was. It hardly seemed to matter.

Once upright, I stumbled around, feeling the wall for the light switch. My hip hit the table with a loud crash and slammed it against the wall.

"Who's there? Who the fuck's there? Answer me! Now!" Kenny's voice thundered through the darkness of the room, and I fumbled for the light switch and flipped it on.

There was Kenny, standing at the end of the mattress, pointing a sawed-off shotgun straight at me. My eyes slammed open with horror as a scream broke free.

"What the hell are you doing?" I yelled at him. "Put that thing down!"

Kenny's face was immobilized with shock, and we both looked around in panic, trying to grasp what just happened. Then my eye caught the mattress.

"Oh my God, Kenny. Look. Look." I pointed to the heap in the bed. Kenny's friend, the lump I had pushed as I was trying to get out of bed, was slumped over, blood trickling out of the corners of his mouth—just like Dale.

"Help him!"

"Holy shit," Kenny said, scrambling to sit his friend up. Trickles of blood had dried in a bizarre pattern on his face, shirtsleeve, and the floor. He didn't appear to be breathing.

"Wake him up. Wake him up. Is he okay? Jesus, Kenny, what are we going to do?"

I was paralyzed with fear. All I could do was stand there and stare. It just couldn't be real.

"For Christ's sake, go and sit down!" Kenny snapped. "Be quiet. He's okay. Just go."

Before I could ask any questions, and while my feet were still anchored to the floor, Kenny flipped the man over his shoulder and they were out the door, a tiny trail of blood spatters the only evidence he had even been there. Suddenly the house was silent. I looked around but saw nothing to indicate what has just happened, other than a few more drops of blood beside the bed. If it weren't for those, I would have thought I had just had a bad dream.

In a trance-like state, I automatically retrieved a wet cloth and began to clean up the spatters of blood. Scrubbing the floor beside the mattress on my hands and knees, I fell in a heap and sobbed. I wasn't sure what I was crying for; I just knew something terrible had happened and that I was part of it.

I was in the same position, clutching the bloody damp cloth, when Kenny returned hours later. My eyes met his, asking the question I was too scared to utter aloud. *Please let him be all right, please.*

"He's fine," Kenny, said, "He just had too much dope, that's all. Took him to the hospital. Don't worry about it." He went to the kitchen and grabbed a beer, but before I could say anything, he glared at me with a look that clearly instructed me to not ask any more questions. We sat beside each other on the mattress, and I watched him drink his beer. I never noticed before just how skinny Kenny himself had become, but sitting beside him, rib to rib, I saw for the first time that his muscles were long gone. Kenny was shrinking. Both of us were just dissolving day by day.

I'd been a witness to death too many times, and I realized that something pivotal had happened. It was time to make some choices about where to go next.

We never spoke about that night again.

"I want to move," I told Kenny one night. It had been several months since the bad night and nothing between us had felt right since.

"What you talkin' about?" he asked, irritated. "We're not moving."

"No, we're not," I said, quietly. "I am."

Kenny looked at me, a look of surprise, tenderness, and sadness, and for a moment I wanted to grab hold of him and assure him I wouldn't really leave.

"We can still see each other," I quickly added. "I just need to have my own space. I can find someplace nearby." But I realized as I spoke that his face had become expressionless.

"Okay." He shrugged like I told him I was going out for groceries.

I rented a room on DuPont Avenue, and Kenny rented the first floor of a house on Selby Street that used to be a funeral home. We would spend time at each other's places just to keep the cops confused. Kenny's place was more like an apartment all to himself, so it was nice to go there and cook and relax.

There were a couple of bikers living there and some hippies, but it wasn't nearly as crazy a scene as I'd been living. Kenny would visit often to get high and hang out, cure weed in the oven, or try to talk me into joining him on a drug deal. But I didn't want anything to do with his business after that last time I'd accompanied him. Besides, I was dealing a lot of heroin myself by that point, which I needed to maintain my habit. But it seemed that no matter how much Street Horse I did, I was always feeling sick. I had hardly any appetite at all and no energy to speak of. But the bikers kept their word. They said they'd always watch out for me, and they did. I still knew that no matter how bad things got, they'd always have my back.

Somehow I found myself in the lobby of a treatment center. I had no memory of how I got there. I couldn't hold any food down, and when I looked in the mirror, the whites of my eyes were the color of dirty lemons. I knew I was sick—real sick.

"Can somebody help me please?" I leaned on the counter of the reception desk for support.

A skinny guy with dirty glasses looked up from the book he was reading.

"You're not old enough to be in here," he said, "You can't have that bad a problem. Come back when you're eighteen. Go on now." He returned to his book with no further comment.

I let Street Horse take me home and comfort me. He galloped wildly through my veins, so carefree and untamed. I laid back and let him play with me. Then he was gone, and the sickness returned.

I knew I needed help, but I didn't know who to tell or who to call. Kenny just said I needed to eat more, but I knew it was more than that. Besides, I had no idea where he was at that time. It might be hours or days before I saw him again, and I needed help fast.

Back on the streets, I headed north and found myself wandering up Spadina Avenue. *Get to the biker house,* I told myself. *They'll help. Get to the guys. Go. Quickly. Go.*

I somehow managed to finally reach the biker house. But before I could raise my hand to knock, the door swung open. I fell into the arms and long, frosty-colored beard of Steve. Steve was an optimist, a happy-go-lucky kind of guy who didn't scare easily. I was so relieved he was the one who opened the door. I could relax. I was safe. I was safe. I was safe.

Steve carried me to the living room and gently plopped me on his plaid couch. I stared at the thick, jagged scar that ran along the side of his left face, the scar he got when someone took a smashed beer bottle to his face. His long, curly dark hair—which he always kept beautifully washed and combed—hung from his head like a soft, dark curtain.

"Quick!" he yelled, "Somebody get her a drink and a blanket. Hurry up." The urgency in his voice frightened me, but I was too weak to do anything but lay back and close my eyes.

Brian stuck his head in the door to see what the yelling was all about.

"Holy shit!" he shouted, "Somebody call Kenny. Fast!" He sounded scared.

Should I be scared? I wondered as I drifted off.

Giant, bearded teddy bears live here, I remember thinking. They would help me. One got a nubby blanket that smelled like beer and wrapped my skeletal body inside it. Another brought me something to drink. Steve held me close, his tattooed arms supporting me as he tried to get me to drink. I said nothing. I had no words. I had no tears. There was nothing left inside me to let out.

As my body relaxed with the reassurance of the teddy bears, I became aware of a terrible pain in my chest.

"Steve," I whispered, "Steve, under my breast, look." I pulled up my top and showed him my swollen abdomen. On the right side, under my breast and along my side, was a swollen area that looked and felt like a rock-hard mango. "It hurts so much," I told him. "What's going to happen to me?" Except for where the swelling was, my ribs protruded from my yellowing skin as if they were asking for help.

Steve placed his massive hand over the mass that had appeared across my lower chest. His touch felt cool and comforting, and I wanted him to leave his hand there forever. When he looked down at me with his deep, dark eyes, I felt as if he were reading my mind, as if he had crawled right through my own eyes and made himself at home in my soul.

"Take it easy, sweetheart. We'll look after you. Don't you worry. Kenny's on his way." He pointed to my eyes and said, "We'll get that sparkle back. You don't look so good in yellow anyway." Steve grinned and held me tight, rocking me in his arms. I managed a weak smile and disappeared into his beard.

Steve fed Street Horse his dinner. I was too weak to even do that. He knew I would be much sicker if they didn't feed him. Every few minutes I struggled to raise my eyelids, only to find several pairs of eyes staring back into mine. If I'd had the energy, I would have laughed. No one would believe such big tough guys, guys who could scare the shit out of you with just one look, could be so tender and caring. They took turns wiping my forehead with cold cloths and feeding me chicken soup straight from the can, all the while holding me close so I wouldn't shiver so much. They reminded me of frightened chickens themselves as they flew around whispering to each other in short bursts of concern.

I was halfway asleep when the front door slammed shut, waking me with a loud bang, and Kenny burst into the living room.

"Holy shit, man. What happened to her?"

"Jesus. You took long enough man," Steve said. "We thought she was gonna die right here."

"Well, shit. Why didn't you just take her to the hospital? What's the matter with you?" Kenny was angry, though I'm not sure if it was because they didn't get me to the hospital or because they interrupted whatever it was he was doing. All I knew was that Kenny was mad.

"Man, she didn't want to go. Said she wanted you to come, that you'd know what to tell 'em. Don't blame me. We did the best we could." Steve was passing the buck to me rather than have Kenny pissed at him.

"Okay. I know you did. Thanks for lookin' after her." Kenny gingerly picked up the blanket-wrapped skeleton that was me, put me in the backseat of a car, and rushed me to St. Michael's Hospital. We didn't talk.

I felt warm breath that smelled like bananas oozing all over my face.

"Open your eyes. Come on. Open them," a strained familiar voice said.

Shit. It can't be her. It can't be her. Please, don't let it be her.

I slowly raised my eyelids and instantly felt the vomit filling my esophagus. It *was* her. It was my mother.

"What the hell are you doing here? Get away from me. Get her out of here!" I screamed.

I tried to push her away, but I was laced to the bed with so many needles and tubes that I could hardly move. As if delighted with my captivity, she leaned closer; her coke-bottle glasses made her eyes look like giant marbles of pure hatred.

With her mouth pinched in a tight line she whispered into my ear, "You deserve this! You should be dead by now. Go ahead. Die. Nobody wants you here." Then she stood up and turned to my father and said crisply, "We should go now."

I'd heard those cruel words before. My eyes closed as I drifted back to the past and remembered all the times she'd said those words. Every time I fell and scraped a knee I was told those words: That I deserved it. That I should have suffered. That nobody wanted me and I should just be gone.

I'll be okay. I'll be okay. I'll be okay.

I prayed for her to be gone, and when I opened my eyes, she was. So was my father. He had stood silently beside her, holding his hat in his two hands and saying nothing.

Weeks later, I felt stronger. I realized how close I had come to dying. But what really shook me up was my mother. Had she really been there? I thought for sure it was just a hallucinogenic nightmare, but as my mind grew more alert, I realized I hadn't imagined it. I couldn't shake the smell of her breath or the hiss of her words; she'd really been there.

The nurses told me that they called her in case I died and they needed to send me somewhere. So she'd just come for my body, and instead she found me alive.

I'm okay. I'm okay. I'm okay.

Swarms of strangers in starched white uniforms passed in and out. They'd burst into my room and poke and prod, talking to each other but not to me. No one ever introduced themselves. I was a broken, wasted body in a bed. I was a medical chart clipped to the bed frame. I was my illness. I was the hepatitis in room 14D.

I wanted to be one of those white coats. I knew if I were one of the white coats, I would talk to patients in a different way, not like that. I would look past the diagnosis and speak to the patient. No one spoke to me. But sometimes they asked the hepatitis if it had had a bowel movement. Sometimes they asked the bed how it was feeling today. Most days they just asked the chart if there were any changes.

As soon as I could stand and walk, I pulled the tubes out of my arms and walked out the door. No one even noticed. I'd put this experience in a drawer in my wall of secrets, I decided.

One of the white coats told me I would die if I didn't stop using Street Horse.

What the hell does he know? I thought. *I'm dead inside already. Hmm, could be a song in there. Haven't thought about songs for a long time.* I couldn't even recall when I'd last played my guitar.

Mother stands behind me with her pointer ready to smack my knuckles as I play.

"Play the right notes. Only those notes, Claire! It has to be perfect or else you might as well not play at all." She hisses the words and spittle lands on top of my head as a warning.

In my mind, I write my own music. That's my
secret.

City time vanished. I had no sense of time; months or years
could have passed, but it was all the same to me. I couldn't get her
voice out of my head. Her voice played in a loop in my head over
and over and over.

*You don't belong here either. You're a child of Satan. You deserve
to die. Nobody will ever love you. Even your own mother didn't want
you. Go away. Nobody wants you.*

Over and over it played. Sometimes I'd wear earplugs to get
rid of her voice. On those days I'd usually feed Street Horse double
dinner, and then her voice was silenced.

*At breakfast a beloved asked her lover, "Who
do you love more, yourself or me?"*
—Rumi

Chapter 9

The Business Man

I see Kenny around town. He's not looking good. He's become skinny, dirty, all jittery, and paranoid—not the Kenny I knew. That makes me sad. I hate what speed does to people. I have a new friend now anyway. His name is Russ, short for Russell. Interesting guy he is, a real businessman, not the street kind. He wants to come to my place all the time. I don't mind. He seems nice enough. He comes over and we just hang out. We listen to my collection of records and feed our Street Horses together. The teddy bears tell me I'm in way over my head and to be careful. I tell them it's okay; I know what I'm doing now. After all, I've been doing this awhile. I'm not a kid any longer. I'm eighteen.

Things were different after my discharge from the hospital. I didn't see much of Kenny, and I made some new friends downtown. "A rough crowd," Biker Steve told me. "Stay away from those guys, Claire. You don't belong with them."

Why is everyone always telling me I don't belong? I wondered. *Someday I'll find the group I belong to, a place where I fit in without having to reshape all the pieces just to make room for a shape like me.*

I met Russell through John. John was a legend from the old village; he was older than my father and had been using heroin since he was a teenager—at least that's what he said. He said it kept him alive. Who knows; maybe it did.

John was sort of like a guru of the streets. Kenny had introduced us, which was a huge thing, because just meeting John was an honor for us kids on the street. He was a recluse, with long, grey hair past his shoulders, and his face was all wrinkled. I found him quite interesting and used to visit him every now and again. He was knowledgeable about so many things, and we liked the same music, so it was always fun to run into him.

Sometimes I would buy from him, though I had no idea where he got his drugs, and I never asked. He wasn't really associated with anyone; he said he liked it better that way.

I was visiting John one afternoon when Russ came by.

Russell was tall, well dressed, and clean-shaven, and he smelled of Old Spice aftershave, something unusual at a time when most guys never showered, much less shaved. His thick, shiny brown hair was cut in a stylish manner, and his clothes were clean and stylish—not at all like the hippies, junkies, and downtowners who all wore the uniform of their culture, whether it was cotton tunics from India or motorcycle leathers. His brown eyes were the same color as mine, and they revealed a deep and sensitive sadness masked by his gentle demeanor. He seemed drawn to me right away, and I was flattered by his attentions. He was different from the rest of the people I knew, and I liked different, since I was pretty different myself.

We quickly became friends. Russ would come to my room, and we would listen to music and do drugs. He would sometimes buy drugs from me to sell to a few customers, just enough to cover his own habit, but he wasn't really a dealer. He had some kind of job in the "real world." He never really spoke about what it was he did, and I never really asked.

Russ was from a small town in Ontario and still spent a lot of time there. We went there every so often and usually stayed in a hotel while he got rid of his drugs, selling them to various friends he knew. One day he surprised me by suggesting we visit his father. His mother had died a few years earlier, but his Dad still lived in the house Russ had grown up in; he wanted to drop by and introduce me to him.

"Really? You're taking me to meet your dad?" I asked with apprehension. No one had ever taken me to meet their parents. Parents were not usually even in the lives of those of us living our street lifestyle.

"Yeah," he said, smiling like an excited little boy. "I have to pick up some things to fix my car, and he wants to meet you. I've told him all about you."

I knew I couldn't get out of it, and a part of me even wanted to go; I wanted to be the girl the guy brought home to his parents. But I knew I was hardly the girl most parents wanted their son to bring home. So I washed my long hair, put on my best jeans, and did my best to look presentable.

As we drove across town, my stomach began rolling over with anxiety. *What would Russell's dad think of me? Would he even like me? What would I say to him? What would we talk about?* The more I thought about it, the more certain I became that his father would deeply resent our arrival—maybe even throw us all out of the house once he saw Russ showing up with his new hippie girlfriend.

"Don't worry," Russ, said, reassuringly, "He's going to love you. Really."

"I sure hope so," I said, though deep down I wished we could turn around and drive straight back to Yorkville.

We soon arrived at a small white house. It was neat and tidy. The yard was tended with manicured shrubs, and weathered oak barrels were filled with flowers.

"This is it. Come on. We'll just have coffee and leave after a bit. He won't bite," Russell said as he opened the car door and reached in to pull me out.

Just as the car door slammed shut, the front door opened. I sucked in a breath and let it out with a whoosh. It had been years since I had met people from the regular world, and I knew he probably wouldn't like me. As cleaned up and eager as I was to impress Russ's dad, there was no denying that I felt out of place just walking into his house.

As the door opened, a hand reached out and grabbed mine, covering it with another hand that was noticeably old, with thick blue veins protruding from wrinkled, spotted skin. His fingernails were short with dirt around the edges and stained yellow from cigarettes.

"Good to meetcha, sweetheart. Come on in! She sure is a pretty girl, Russell," he said, babbling enthusiastically as we stood on the porch. As he was pumping my arm up and down, his dull gray eyes stared into mine as if he were peering into my soul. Shivers rippled up my spine and along my arms, leaving goose bumps, and I felt chilled to the bone.

"Come on, come on in," he said, showing a toothy, dentured grin. "Finally, I get to meet the woman of my son's heart. I've heard so much about you. Come on in." His hand still clutched mine as he pulled me up the few stairs to the front door. Russ was behind me, giving me a little push, as if he was afraid I wouldn't budge. I turned around and he nodded and grinned, as if to say, "Yes, go on and go inside."

The truth was I was shocked by his father's words. I had no idea that Russ had been telling his dad anything about me. I didn't know if I should feel flattered or frightened; all I knew was I had better be on guard. They ushered me into the front hallway and then we went into the living room.

"I'll get some coffee. You just sit," Russ's dad said, heading to the kitchen. The living room was well worn but tidy. There were touches only a woman would make. Little white doilies sat on the side tables holding candy jars full of humbugs. Framed family photos were clustered together on the mantle. Magazines were piled up on the wooden coffee table along with a tall ceramic bluebird sitting on its doily seat. It seemed like it was staring directly at me, and it gave me the creeps. I reached over and discretely turned it around.

"My mom made that," Russ said. "Pretty good, eh? See that picture on the table over there in the silver frame? That's her with Dad on their twenty-fifth anniversary."

"She's beautiful," I said, not quite sure how to respond since she had passed away. "You must miss her."

"I sure do. She was good to us kids. Then she got really sick and the doctors couldn't figure out what was wrong. It was awful. It went on for quite a while, and then eventually she just died."

"Did she have cancer?" I asked gently. He hadn't discussed his mother's death much in the past.

"No, no she didn't. The doctors could never figure out what it was, and then one day she just died." He stared at the picture with a sadness I hadn't seen before, and I realized Russ had been holding a great deal of pain inside him for a very long time. I wondered what it must have felt like to be loved by a mother so much and what it must have felt like to lose her at such a young age.

"I'm sorry, Russ," I said, reaching for his hand. He put his arm around me just as his dad returned with two mugs of coffee.

"Didn't know what you took, so I put it all in. Sugar and cream okay?" he asked, carefully setting down the hot, steamy mugs on round coasters with cats on them. "My wife, she loved cats," he said, noticing me looking at the plastic coasters.

"Oh, that's nice. Thank you for the coffee," I said, snuggling closer to Russ, unsure why I felt so uneasy.

I looked around the living room while Russ and his dad rambled on about car parts and gossiped about family members I didn't know. Bird figurines were scattered around the room, each on its own little doily, some with frills around the edges. Over the mantle was a lovely painting of an autumn river scene, hung in a faded gold-gilt frame. A road ran along the river, and I imagined I'd like to get up and walk right out of the room and down that road, with Heart Horse by my side.

I missed Heart Horse.

"Claire, Claire? It's time we left." Russ said, nudging my shoulder and drawing my attention back to the continuing conversation about cars. "Sorry if we're boring you! We're just going to the garage to get some tools I need, and then we gotta get going." He smiled sweetly as I quickly assured him that they weren't boring me at all. I was enjoying the conversation; I'd never realized there was so much to know about carburetors and pistons.

We followed his father out to the garage, which was as cold as a deep freeze. As Russ sorted through a box of tools and chatted with his dad about which ones he could take with him, I glanced over and noticed his father smiling strangely at me, while looking me up and down like a three-piece suit he'd like to try on for size.

"Found it!" Russ said, pulling out a greasy wrench. "Okay, let's go; it's getting late. We'll come back another time, Dad."

"Nice girl ya got there, Russ," his dad said while staring into my eyes. "You be good to her, ya here?"

Then his dad came up to me and pressed his body close against mine, wrapping his arms around me in a lascivious hug that felt so wrong I instantly stiffened. My arms hung straight at my sides, and I tried to step back to give some distance between us as he pulled me even closer so he could cop a quick and discreet feel of my breasts. Relief flooded me as he let me go and we were soon out the door and into the warm sunshine.

Sitting in the car I felt safe again. With a quick wave and a shudder, we were on our way home—back to Toronto where I was safe.

The drive was quiet. Unspoken words filled the car with questions from both of us. Questions neither of us was ready to answer.

The mind is its own place, and itself can make
a heaven of hell, a hell of heaven.
—John Milton

Chapter 10

Into the Rabbit Hole

Yonge Street was always busy. The subways were always packed. The stores were always full. I would go there to sit and watch. I watched for eyes—eyes like mine.

People avoided my eyes. They knew my stares were full of questions. They quickly looked in the other direction. Did they know I was only searching for myself? I was only searching for a pair of eyes that would look back at me and recognize me at once—a pair of eyes that would say, "I've found you. You belong with me."

I searched for eyes that looked like mine and wondered if the mother who didn't want me would be hiding behind a pair of them.

Heart Horse just stood by quietly. We had no fight left in either of us.

My skin always felt clammy, even in the sweltering summer heat. The city air was soaked with smog, suffocating me with every breath. After walking a few blocks, my face would be covered with the grime and grit of the city sky. I would blow my nose and notice the black slime like squid ink left behind in the tissue.

I walked mostly at night. The middle of the night had always been my favorite time to think. The streets were raw and quiet then, and my mind ran free in the silence of a darkened world.

It was another night of dealing, another night of Street Horse galloping through my veins. I followed the lights flickering on and off, showing me the way home, hoping that one day one light would guide me—just one light to illuminate my path. Was this the night? I looked up to the sky, hoping to see a galaxy of stars, but all I could see was a blanket of grey. There would be no guiding light that night.

I opened my door just as the sun began its rise. All I wanted was a hot bath to erase the city's grime and soak away the memories. In the tub, steamy water built a bubble cover over my legs. Scooping up the hot suds, I covered my face in a white cloud. As I scraped off the foam with my fingers, I counted my battle wounds, the ones that had left pathways in my skin. Seven. Seven scars had seared their stories into my flesh. One sliced across my hand where Mother hit me with the music pointer and my skin split. Another one sat at the base of my hairline from when she caught me from behind with the hand mirror. The last one was over my eyebrow. It was from the time I fell and hit my head. Seven stitches left that trail.

Lost in thought, I let my body slip under the water as I imagined I was floating in a mountain lake. I waited to feel myself relax and connect with the universe, as if I were a part of the universal clockworks, as much a part of the world as the air and the earth.

If every element of nature is inherently perfect, I reasoned, *might I be as well? Am I not every bit a part of nature, as much as a worm or a butterfly? Do I not have a function, a role to play in the world, as much as any other?*

I floated in the tub, my private mountain lake, my eyes closed and my mind dreaming. I was dreaming of a mountain landscape, a crystal lake, an iridescent sky—a land of wild horses.

There was a time when I thought my life would truly be spent in the mountains, floating on a lake. I thought my life would take me to the mountains where I would find and care for a wild horse of my own. Sadly, it had become a Street Horse that I'd found and cared for.

I spent all my time with Street Horse now. Even Heart Horse had given up. Yet for a moment, floating in the warm, soapy water with my eyes closed, I could have sworn I felt the soft and unmistakable stirrings of Heart Horse deep inside. I let my mind linger in the mountains of my mind, savoring memories of grassy smells and crisp, clean air, Heart Horse by my side. Just beyond our reach, just beyond our view, I knew the wild horses waited.

Bam, bam, bam! A loud knock interrupted my thoughts.

"Hey, whatcha doing in there? Ya been in there long enough, don'tcha think? Get the hell out, will ya!" a gruff voice ordered. It was Joey. Joey lived upstairs. Six of us shared the bathroom.

"Yeah, yeah. Just be another minute. Hold your horses," I replied.

The bathroom had filled with steam, and I hated to leave its warm embrace, but I knew my time was up. I tried to dry off with my flimsy towel. But no matter how much I rubbed, it seemed my body stayed damp from the steam. Taking my towel to the mirror, I rubbed in a circular motion until I made a round hole in the steam.

I don't know who you are anymore. Where is the old me?

A stranger stared back at me. She had the same long hair, the same scars as I did, but her face was sunken in and her eyes were hollow. My face wasn't like that. I was young and pretty. The stranger asked the same questions as I asked her. My eyes thickened and turned red, and hers did the same. Tears leaked from my eyes, and hers did the same. I swiped at the tears, and she did the same. She could feel my pain so that I didn't need to.

It was time to go feed Street Horse.

I erased the last of the steam-mirror girl and wrapped my towel around my damp body. I tiptoed back to my room, and as soon as I got behind the safety of my door, I began the familiar ritual with spoon and water. Getting dressed could wait.

Just as I pulled the thick leather string tightly around my arm, my bedroom door crashed open and an explosion of noise, confusion, and screaming blew into the room. Two men in dark suits grabbed my arms and threw me onto the bed. My wet towel fell on the floor, and I was stark naked as two big men stood over me with faces fixed in fury. In an instant, my room filled with angry cops—some in blue, some in suits, some with beards and blue jeans. All of them stopped to stare at my naked body on the bed, each with the same grin on their face.

"Get your fucking hands off of me, you assholes!" I shouted at the cops.

"Shut up. Where is it?" Brown Suit said.

"Where's what? I don't know what you're talking about." I tried to pull the bedspread over my body but his hands tightened their grip. He wanted to see me humiliated, to see me squirm.

A big guy with a beard flipped me over and pulled one of my arms far back behind me and twisted it hard.

"It's easier if you just tell us," he said as he twisted my bones like he was tightening the lid on a jar. Not even the Para-Dice assholes had been as cruel.

"I don't know what you're talking about! Let go of my arm, you pig!" I replied, wincing from the excruciating pain.

He leaned over with his nose practically touching mine. The stench of stale cigarettes mixed with scotch oozed from his mouth and flooded mine.

"Give it up, now," he ordered. He pulled his other arm back, exposing growing patches of sweat under his arms. They were in the shape of Italy.

With a fast swipe, the back of his hand hit my lip and it burst open, spurting blood directly onto his sweaty white T-shirt. I smiled to myself thinking how he wouldn't want any blood evidence to be on him. But it was an impotent smile. In an instant, everything in my world had shattered, and all I could do was sit naked and watch it happen as warm blood oozed from my mouth and down the side of my face.

A tall guy in blue cautioned, "Take it easy with her. You don't want any marks showing when we take her in."

"Yeah, yeah. Won't do anything that shows," Bearded Guy said with a smirk as he stuck his tongue into my ear. My leg swung up instinctively and smashed his shin. "You little bitch," he said as he yanked me up by my tortured arms and swung me onto my feet. "You might as well just tell us. We're going to find it one way or the other."

"I don't know what you want," I cried, "Anything here is just my personal shit. Leave me alone!" As I looked around the demolished room, I shivered. "Can I get dressed? At least give me my robe. I can charge you too, you know, for sexual assault."

The blue-jeaned cop with the Italy-stained T-shirt just laughed then pulled my arms behind me and snapped a pair of cuffs around my wrists. They were so tight that if I moved even an inch, my skin would tear. He put his gorilla arm around my naked waist and reached his other gorilla arm across and grabbed my breast. I squirmed to twist out of his grip, but the more I fought him, the tighter he gripped me.

"Got it. Hey, I got it. I knew we'd find it," Brown Suit announced. Everyone stopped in midsentence and movement and stared at him. Even Gorilla Arms stopped hurting me. Brown Suit held up a large bag of Street Horse and another bag with gelatin capsules, smiling victoriously like he was holding up a trophy.

"Hey. That's not mine!" I screamed. "No way. I don't have that much. I don't know where that came from! You gotta believe me!"

My mind swirled in confusion as I tried to figure out where that shit could have come from. I'd only had enough for a few hits, but they were holding up half an ounce or more. Cops were known to plant drugs, and wherever that had come from, I knew one thing: it wasn't mine.

Gorilla Arms gripped my crotch in glee, his fingers digging into my flesh. I tried jabbing my elbows into his soft ugly belly, but with every move, he tightened his grip.

"Pig," I whispered.

"Shut up, bitch," he whispered into my ear. "You're getting what you deserve." He tightened his grip. I gritted my teeth. I'd be damned if I would let him see how much I hurt.

She was standing beside me as I sat in my dad's chair at the head of the table. Her words were hurled like poisonous darts, each one slamming into the side of my head. Suddenly, her hand flew out of nowhere, and it felt like my head was going to fly off with the force. But I didn't even wince. I just turned my head and stared into her unfeeling eyes.

"Well, don't you have anything to say for yourself?" she asked me.

In answer, I said nothing. Slowly rising from my dad's chair, I left the room as she continued her verbal attack.

She can't hurt me anymore. Not now. Not later. I will talk someday. Not now, but someday. That's my secret.

"Okay. We have enough. Take her out," Brown Suit said.

"Throw some clothes on her," the tall cop ordered.

"Nah, she don't need no clothes; just throw a blanket on her," Gorilla Arms said. A blanket was thrown at me, and with one on each side, the cops whisked me out and into their waiting squad car. I thought for sure that they were going to take me somewhere and hurt me, so I was actually thankful when we got to the jail.

At least I'm safe, for now, I thought, *but not forever.*

I was charged with intent to traffic, conspiracy to import, and trafficking heroin.

Somehow, out of one crime, they'd created three crimes— thinking about it, talking about it, and doing it. It was a wonder they didn't charge me with remembering I'd done it. Though to be fair, the heroin they were charging me with trafficking I had never even seen before, so I could only remember the crimes I wasn't charged with, not the crimes I was charged with.

I got word to Kenny to take care of my things, and he promised he would, but after that, I didn't hear from him. I didn't hear from anyone for that matter. Once I was thrown in jail, life went on without me out on the streets.

But inside, weeks disappeared without my seeing daylight. Most days were spent with my head leaning against the cold metal bowl they called a toilet. My muscles ached and would quiver in spasms. The dirty mattress they called a bed was stained and torn in places.

My sweat and tears dissolved in the stains of many others before me. It was impossible to rest.

The jail was disgusting. On one of my first nights there, I leaned over the hole to vomit and was met by a huge nasty looking rat as big as a cat. He was glistening black with slime and smelled like a sewer. He sat on his haunches, snarling to show his teeth, his huge yellow eyes staring right at me in flagrant defiance. At first I thought I was hallucinating, but when I screamed, the girl in the next cell said she saw them too.

"Sewer rats," she explained. "Here all the time."

Rats from the Don River. It flowed right beside and under the jail. I'd just have to get used to them, just have to shut them out of my mind.

> I hate going to the basement. Hate it. Hate it. Hate it. I know when she makes me go there that there is always the chance she'll make me go in the root cellar. It's always me she sends in there to get potatoes or apples. She knows I'm afraid she's going to do what she did before. It's so musty and dark, and the rats stick their heads out of the little pipe at the top of the ceiling. I've seen them with my own eyes. There were so many of them that time before. But I try not to think about that time.

I'd never been that sick, not even in the hospital. But no one was taking care of me; they ignored you in jail. As they patrolled the halls, the guards would stop, stare in my cell, chuckle, and say I got what I deserved.

No one deserves to be treated like an animal, I thought. I really wanted to die.

"Hey, get up. Put this on right now." Matron opened the door with a clang. "Come on, hurry up. You got court," she said, laughing as she threw a stiff blue uniform dress and black shoes on the floor of the cell. "Come on, girl. You'll look real pretty. Ya got five minutes to shower."

She led me down the hall to the communal shower room. The shower was comprised of five showerheads lined up in a row and surrounded by bars. Usually everybody was in there together, but standing there alone, with Matron watching me closely, I felt more exposed than if the shower room were packed with prisoners. I quickly lathered the bar soap into my hair. It was matted and crunchy where the sweat and vomit has dried over the last few days. Every muscle was shaky. What energy I had left was washed down the drain with the dirty gray water. I had just enough time to cover myself with a layer of soap when suddenly the water was shut off.

"Are you kidding me? Turn the water back on!" I snapped. "Hey, Matron. Hey, bitch. Turn it on!" My voice echoed down the hall, matching the clumpy footsteps of Matron heading my way. Her steps grew louder.

"I told ya. Five minutes. That's it. You're done."

I stood in a puddle of soap slime in disbelief. I was covered in drying soap.

"Come on!" I yelled, "Turn it on, goddammit! I can't go like this."

Without warning, my feet flew out from under me. I grabbed at the air as if it would stop my fall. I landed on my back with a loud thud, one of my feet skidding under the metal rail.

Blood pooled under my foot. The sharp edges of the rail had sliced through the top of my foot like a knife. I could see my own bone.

"Get me out of here," I said, struggling to hold my foot together. "Come on!"

"What the hell did you do now? Get up, for Christ's sake. Come on. Now!" Matron stood on the other side of the shower bars, smirking as if entertained by my pain. "You gotta get to court. Move it."

"Are you kidding me? Look," I replied. I pointed to the red river of blood that had begun snaking across the floor, lifting my foot a few inches higher so she could see the blood.

The soap had already begun to dry, pulling my skin taught and turning my hair into a nasty clump of strings. Blood was pouring out of the slice, and as I stood up, it opened even wider.

"I don't think I can walk on it," I said.

"You're going to court, so get out and get dressed," she replied.

She opened the shower room door with a loud clang and slammed it shut again as she pushed and shoved me along. I could barely put my toes on the floor. Any movement caused blood to spurt out, leaving a sanguine trail behind me. She grabbed my arm and pulled me faster, ignoring my protests and winces. When we got to my cell, she pushed me inside and slammed the door.

"Five minutes. That's all ya get," she grunted.

The thin towel was soaked with a mixture of blood and soap, but I tried to dry myself off as best as I could. I had no underwear. I had no socks. My hands were shaky as I tried to button the front of my dress. A puddle of blood pooled beneath my foot.

"Oh, crap," Matron said. She was staring at my foot and the expanding puddle spreading across the floor. "Come on. You'll have to get stitches. No court for you today," she said, clearly irritated at the inconvenience I had caused her.

In minutes I was standing outside, snow covering my sockless feet. My damp, blue uniform dress stiffened in the freezing air. Long strings of soapy hair had become crispy. Matron threw a black jacket over my shoulders. It smelled of mothballs and mold. One push and I fell headfirst into the back seat of a bright yellow cab. My blue dress was embarrassingly short, and I tried to pull it down as the taxi driver watched in the mirror, the spit in his half-opened mouth glistening on his brown-stained teeth. He reminded me of one of the rats. I gave him my best fuck-off look and he smiled, still watching.

"St. Michaels Hospital," Matron ordered as she got in beside me.

"Sure thing," the taxi man said, his eyes glued to the mirror.

I said nothing. My tears had frozen in a layer of soap, my humiliation considered deserved.

I winced as I climbed up onto the examining table. Matron stood motionless beside me, unwilling to help as she reveled in the power of her uniformed role. The nurses laughed when I told them how this happened, and Matron laughed with them.

I tried to settle myself neatly on the table. My dress barely covered my thighs. The hot tears brimmed over my eyes.

This is all so wrong, I thought. *I'm so embarrassed.*

I felt Heart Horse nudge his nose beneath my ribs, comforting me with his warm and loving breath.

> At one of the church suppers, an old lady that looked like a cartoon character sat across from me. My mother sat beside me, staring out of the corner of her eye to make sure I was sitting properly, my back straight and my hands in my lap.
>
> "Pull your dress down!" she ordered me, and I tugged at my hem, but there was no way to make the hemline longer. My father was on my other side, anticipating all of the home-cooked goodies.

"Why, Claire! You are looking more like your daddy every time I see you," Cartoon Lady says.

"No. No, I'm not!" I snap back. I'm ad—" But before I can finish my sentence, my mother cuts in.

"Claire, enough or you'll have to leave the table!" Mother says as she squeezes my arm until it bleeds where her nails dig in. I flush in embarrassment and look down at my empty plate, knowing what I really wanted to say. Not now, but someday. Someday, I'll tell everyone. That's my secret.

My body shook with a chill that had nothing to do with the temperature.

"Do you think I could have a blanket?" I asked.

Matron smiled and shook her head. "What for? You ain't got nothin' the doc hasn't seen before."

A young doctor came into the room, holding a clipboard. He looked at me and then at Matron and then back at me.

"Nasty foot you have there," he said as he sat down at the end of the table. "Won't take long." He opened his tray and set about arranging his equipment. His eyes avoided mine.

I struggled to keep my legs together and my dress pulled down. Each time I closed my legs, he moved my foot back to the outside of the table.

"Leave it there," he instructed, still without making eye contact. A sudden flash of Randy and the Mohawk grabbing hold of me, ordering me into position, passed before me and I froze. The doctor grabbed my foot, spreading my bare legs open as he pushed the foot to the side. He raised his stool and began sewing my flesh.

"Aren't you going to freeze it first?" I asked as he swabbed the top of my foot.

"No. Don't think you need it. I'll be quick," he replied, his eyes on my foot.

I closed my eyes and pretended I was somewhere else. I was a piece of meat to be stitched up, nothing more. Matron shifted back and forth on her feet. Even she had become uncomfortable.

As quickly as they delivered me to the hospital, I was returned to my cell. Without any conversation, Matron shoved me into my cage, pulling the door shut with a purposeful clang. I sat in shock, wondering if it had all been a dream. I was still covered in dried soap mixed with blood and tears, and my bandaged foot was throbbing, so it had to be real.

After some time, Matron returned, this time laughing.

"While you were flirting with that doctor, the court went ahead and sealed your fate," she said. "Found you guilty, honey, guilty as sin!" Then she turned and walked away, chuckling to herself like she'd just been told the funniest thing.

"Bitch," I said as I watched her disappear. Heart Horse nuzzled me gently.

It's okay, it's okay, it's okay.

I'll be fine, I'll be fine, I'll be fine.

I circled the dress buttons over and over with my pointer finger as I said my mantras—over and over and over.

Most of the shadows of this life are caused by
our standing in our own sunshine.
—Ralph Waldo Emerson

Chapter 11

Musical Ride

One of my friends said it was a set up. Russ was in on it, he said, and turned me in to avoid jail himself after a big deal went bad and he got pulled in by the cops. It made sense. I had thought we were friends, but it was the only explanation that made sense. He disappeared after the bust, I was told.

I was sentenced to two years less one day for each of the charges, and they were to run concurrently. What that meant was that instead of six years, I'd serve two years (less a day). Because it was one day less than two years, it was considered a provincial offense; rather than going to the maximum security federal penitentiary, I would go to the minimum security women's facility where I would have my own room and much more freedom to move around and mingle with people.

It would also mean I would not be going with the friends who'd been busted with me. When I was thrown in the squad car, all I had thought about was it was all happening to me. But after I'd been arrested, I learned they'd busted the whole house and a lot of other people as well.

So no matter how much easier my sentence was to be, which the judge explained was due to my young age, all I could think of was that once again I didn't belong. They'd be together; I'd be kept out. I'd serve my sentence alone.

And so it was that I began my sentence feeling furious—not at the sentence but at the separation from my new friends I'd met in jail and the old from outside. My anger did nothing to endear me to the staff, but anger was the only emotion I felt safe with. Any other emotion led to disappointment or defeat.

Days passed. I stopped vomiting, my muscles stopped aching, I was feeling stronger, and my foot was healing. I took the stitches out myself.

Weeks passed. I tried to follow the rules. I got a job in the prison laundry and learned how to dry-clean clothes. I enrolled in some classes, in hopes that even though they didn't provide any way to earn a high school diploma while incarcerated, I could at least make progress toward that goal.

A few months went by without incident. I made new friends, but I especially got close to Nicky. Nicky was tall and skinny with short blonde hair she kept slicked back. Every inch of her visible skin was stained in tattoos. When she smiled, she revealed a gaping hole where bottom teeth should have been. She said they were knocked out in a fight. She played the most beautiful guitar music. You would have never imagined a girl like Nicky could play such hauntingly beautiful melodies filled with words that made my heart cry, but she did.

As Heart Horse slowly returned to life, he swayed and trotted in delight whenever she played.

One day an announcement was made that some popular local musicians were coming in to do a workshop. I could sense the excitement buzzing through the groups. Many of us played instruments when we weren't doing assigned duties. Piano and guitar were the most popular. I had barely noticed the absence of music in my life after moving to Toronto; music had died inside me when I found Street Horse. But now I realized how much I really missed it. It was funny how the very dreams that brought me to the city were the dreams that were the very first to be extinguished once I got there.

When the musicians arrived, we were assigned to small groups after our workday. Jay was the leader of the group. He reminded me of my biker friends, big and gruff with a wild beard and hair to his shoulders, but with a gentle spirit. He was the one who was most well known. His friend Daryl played the piano, and she played it beautifully. She didn't play professionally very often because she was also a law student, she explained, and wanted a career where she could make a difference and help people like us.

Jay and Daryl wanted to change lives with their music. They wanted to change the world—and not just by writing and singing about society's problems. They came through the prison gates to actually help us with our problems.

"Claire, can you show us something on your guitar?" Daryl asked me. Daryl was a tall, slender woman with thick, curly black hair that hung to her shoulders. She had a slight overbite and a prominent Jewish nose (which I really liked, because mine was shaped a lot like it). Her voice was so kind and tender that I thought she must have been half angel.

I had written a new song, but I was terribly self-conscious about playing it in front of them. However, I forced myself to do it. As I was playing, Jay joined in on his guitar, and then Daryl began picking up the melody on her piano. The group was playing my song! I was surrounded by my own music and could hardly believe my ears. It was utterly surreal to think these well-known musicians were playing *my* music right alongside me. I was in heaven.

Before they left, Daryl approached me and said, "You play very beautifully. Have you had training?"

"Only when I was a kid, and only in piano," I said, wincing at the memories of my mother forcing me to play for hours, hitting me each time I hit a wrong note or was otherwise less than perfect.

"Well, you have a real talent, Claire. I hope you'll keep writing your songs."

"My heart holds many songs," I wrote in my journal that afternoon. "Maybe my spirit isn't broken after all. And maybe Nicky's isn't either."

I couldn't wait for them to return. I worked extra hard in the laundry. I made extra trips for coffee for the guards and swept and scrubbed until my knuckles were raw meat. I didn't want anything to come in the way of my spending time with the group when they returned, so I did everything to ensure I wouldn't be hassled by the guards whenever Joe and Daryl came for the weekly workshops.

Writing music made the weeks fly past, and playing with Jay and Daryl were the highlights of my life. For the first time in my life, I felt that maybe I had a genuine purpose; maybe I really was special, maybe even gifted.

"You're very talented, Claire," Daryl told me almost every time we had a workshop. "You really should pursue this when you get out."

"Really? Do you think I'm good enough for that?" I'd ask her, always thrilled to hear her reply.

"I think you're even better!" And she'd smile like a guardian angel, soft and full of love. And deep inside me, I felt Heart Horse smiling as well.

Then one day, without warning, a bulletin appeared on the board announcing the final concert of the group.

"Holy crap. It can't be. Nicky, did you see this?" I asked, pulling her off her feet.

"I know. Too bad, eh? Good while it lasted," Nicky replied, and then she noticed me. I completely fell apart. "Hey, Claire, it's okay," Nicky said, her strong hands holding my shoulders as they convulsed with sobs.

"It always happens," I replied in between sobs. "Anything good always gets taken away."

I broke from her grip and ran to my room. I was embarrassed to be so emotional in front of everyone. I hadn't cried in a long time.

> The books, the pictures, the library with my wall of secrets, all are gone. Even the doll Grandma gave me. The scarf my friend Wendy gave me. The awards I won at school. They're all gone.
>
> "I don't care if you want then or like them, you can't have them." Mother always said that.
>
> I don't tell her anymore when I like something. That's my secret.
>
> I'm okay. I'm okay. I'm okay.

I took a deep breath and accepted the truth: I didn't belong in their music group either. As I rolled over, I shoved my new secret into a drawer where I wouldn't have to think about it anymore.

At dinnertime Nicky came looking for me. She understood that I wasn't just upset about a workshop ending; she knew it meant much more than that to me. Her clear blue eyes were filled with concern as she held out a hand.

"Hey, girl, it'll be okay. Really." She tried her best to coax me into a good mood, but I was stubbornly set on feeling sorry for myself. "Hey, guess what?" Nicky said. Her tone changed to a happy one. "I'm getting out! By the end of the week! Can you believe it?"

I tried to smile as happily as I could, but it was hard to feel much joy for Nicky's release. She'd be leaving me too.

"That's great, Nicky, that's really cool," I said, "But I'm sure going to miss you."

"Don't worry; you'll be out soon too—before you even know it! You can come and see me when you get out. We'll play music together, you and me," she said, pulling me upright.

"Sure," I replied. "We can do that."

I didn't go to the final concert. I didn't want anyone to see my sadness of yet another ending.

Nicky said the concert was amazing. Jay left his new album for us to play.

"Oh, and Daryl left you this letter," Nicky said. She smiled as she pulled a neatly folded piece of paper from her pocket. My hand shot out with lightning speed and grabbed it from her.

"Sorry and thanks," I said as I stuffed it, unread, into my back pocket.

It was against the rules for visitors to fraternize with us, so Daryl couldn't come to see me personally. But she knew she could trust Nicky. I patted my pocket just to reassure myself that Daryl's message was really there. Passing notes was against the rules, and I knew if anyone saw me with it, it could be snatched away, possibly even before I'd had a chance to read it. It would have to wait until lights out, when I'd sneak a look in the privacy of my room.

I had a hard time carrying on any conversation during dinner and prayed for an early lights out. But it never came. It seemed like an eternity before I finally had a chance to read Daryl's note. Once

95

I was locked in my room for the night, I pulled it out. My fingers trembled as I tore open the paper and brought it to my nose to smell. The musicians were always surrounded by incense, jasmine, and sandalwood. I wondered if I could smell it on the paper, but I couldn't. Still, I closed my eyes and imagined those exotic smells as if they were Daryl herself. Inside, her words were written in purple ink. She wrote a long and loving note and at the very end, she added: "You are a great person and a wonderful musician. I want to keep in touch. Call me when you get out."

Daryl had written her phone number at the bottom in big block numbers. I read the note over and over until it was memorized and locked in my heart forever. Then I wrote the number on my arm, went into the bathroom, and tore the letter into tiny squares, flushing them all away, never to be discovered. Scrambling back into bed, I dug out my journal and wrote the number backward on different pages. The guards read our journals every day, so we learned to always put things in code.

Heart Horse galloped excitedly around in my chest. My eyes refused to stay shut, and my mind was spinning with fantasies of my near future. But the more excited I became, the more demons of doubt jostled for attention, trying to gobble up any positive ideas about the backward number I'd written down. The demons wanted to spit back my hopeful imaginings and replace them with doom and doubt. After all, who was I to think such an incredible and accomplished person as Daryl would want to see me? Letting myself enjoy her attentions and interest in my music would only bring me pain.

That night I tossed and turned waiting for daylight, which seemed light years beyond. Daryl's note had given me hope, and it had been a long time since I'd had that. But my excitement was dampened by my fears. Did I dare have any hope at all? Or would hope for anything, anything good at all just set me up for disappointment?

> She said I could go! I'm so excited. Every year I asked to go to camp, and every year she said no. All my friends went, and when they got back, it's all they talked about. But this year she said yes!
>
> When it was time to turn the money in, she said, "Oh that. I forgot to tell you. You have to go with us to the lake and help with the canning again this year. You eat the food, so you have to help preserve it. We can't do all the work, you know." She smiled with only one side of her lips as she said it. She knew the hurt she was causing; it even pleased her to inflict it. Once she knew I wanted something, she always took it away.
>
> Someday I'll do something I want, have something I want, wear something I want. Not right now, but someday. That's my secret.

Eventually, after short, troubling bursts of sleep, a new day began. In prison there is no accounting of time. It slips into the atmosphere like the marshmallow clouds that roll over the buildings, and you learn to just be ready to do what they said, when they said it, with or without a good night's rest. I was facing one of those days.

The next day was a Saturday, but that meant nothing. We had work detail seven days a week. I opened the door to go to the kitchen to prepare the coffee when I heard a familiar laugh.

It can't be. It can't be. It can't be.

As I turned the corner into the kitchen, I saw a friend from downtown, Shelly, standing with her arms wide open and a grin just as wide to match. Shelly was a legend in the downtown Toronto scene, and she was one of the first people I had met when I came to the city. I couldn't believe she was actually standing there.

"It's you! It's really you! Oh my God, it's good to see you!" I babbled awkwardly. "What happened? What are you doing here?"

"Come on, girl, give me a hug before they see," Shelly replied, laughing.

We danced around in the hallway giddy with excitement.

"I've been at Kingston," she explained, referring to the Kingston Federal Penitentiary. "But there was a little trouble there, and they shipped me here. Man, it's so good to see you."

We knew our every move would be watched since the guards knew we were friends, so we pulled away from each other's embrace and calmed down. Besides, little red flags were rearing their ugly little heads, no matter how forcefully I tried to stomp them back down. Why was she really there? Did I dare risk trusting her? Would the guards punish us for being happy? It wasn't so easy to keep the doubts down without the help of Street Horse, but I had no choice.

I'll just ignore them, I decided, while Heart Horse whinnied in the distance, nervous and alert.

Prison life fell back into its routine. Guards bossed us around, a few groped and leered, and friendships were made. Discharge promises to reconnect were whispered. People came and went; some soon returned. Nicky was released and never did return. I heard that she died a week after she got home. We would never play music together again.

The days that followed were lonely and long. Mariel and her husband, the friends of my mother's when I first left home, came by to visit me once but never again. My parents didn't visit, and my friends didn't visit, not that I expected them to. Russell was long gone, and I hadn't heard a word from Kenny. At least I knew he was keeping my things safe. I didn't want to lose my guitar.

I went up for parole a couple of times, but both times they denied it. They said I wasn't ready, wasn't trying hard enough, had no plans.

What kind of plans can I make now? Where do I even start? I wondered, but they didn't get it.

Christmas came, but most of us didn't have any family who'd visit, and we wanted to forget about the normal festivities. They put up a tree and decorations anyway, which only made us sad. We were hanging decorations when a screech blasted through the room.

"Oh my God! Come quick. You have to see this. Hurry," Shelly said. "It's Russ. Your Russ."

"*My* Russ? What do you mean? Shit," I replied as I dropped on the couch to watch.

They were interviewing Russell on television on the front lawn of his dad's house, while behind him, police were taking his father away in handcuffs. Russ spun around and watched the cops walk his dad to a squad car, and then his dad looked up and stared straight ahead into the television camera. His dull gray eyes stared straight into mine, as if he were looking directly at me. I had to blink several times to clear my vision. Russell's dad was wearing an unmistakable smirk as they shoved him into a waiting squad car.

The newsman said that Russ's father had been arrested for poisoning Russ's mother. They had received a tip, dug up her body, and found she'd been killed from arsenic. Russ went to his dad and got a confession out of him for the police—and then he tried to kill him.

Mother murdered by father. Father almost murdered by son. I couldn't process it. To think I had spent time at his father's house.

Russ's framing me was nothing compared to what could have happened had I stayed with him and gotten close to that family.

"Shit, girl. I told you he was bad," Shelly said. "You're lucky to be alive."

"I know. I can't believe it," I replied.

On the surface I looked calm. Inside, I was confused and frightened—first Randy then Kenny, and then Russell.

Who were these men I allowed into my heart and life? I wondered, as I sat stunned on the prison couch.

"Come on, let's finish this tree," Shelly said, handing me a box of gold plastic bells.

I hung each one in silence.

"There, on the left, by the red bulb. Put one there," Mother orders as she points to where she wants it. I gently drape the worn-out silver tinsel— painstakingly saved and recycled year after year until it was brittle with age—over the branch she has pointed to then move to the next branch.

"Over there, beside the blue ball," she instructs, her long, red-polished fingers pointing to the exact spot she wants it placed. As I reach out and slowly drape the tinsel over the branch, a hand suddenly smacks mine and the blue ball and silver tinsel crash to the floor. The ball shatters instantly, pieces of paper-thin glass flying everywhere. I have no idea where the tinsel went.

"I put it where you said," I whisper, angry and humiliated once again.

"No. No, you did not," she says. "I knew you wouldn't do it right. Clean up that mess. Clean it up and get out of here. Now!"

As I go to get the broom and dustpan, I cry, but without any tears. I know I can do it right. And I will someday, when I have my own tree. Someday. But not today. Today's been broken.

Nights brought terror. Locked away, Street Horse denied me, there was nothing to block the memories of my mother. Seeing Russell's dad being led away for murdering his mother was like having a giant rock thrown through my brain. *Why had Russell's good mother died and my bad mother lived? What was so awful about her that her own husband would kill her—not just in one, angry blow, but in meal after meal, drink after drink, for weeks, months maybe, killing her over and over? What if my own mother dies one day and is dug back up out of the earth? Would she never stay buried?*

She could intrude at any time. Sometimes I had dreams so real I couldn't tell which part was just a dream and which had really happened to me. I'd sit bolt upright, covered in a layer of sweat, Heart Horse racing uncontrollably, banging into my rib cage as my tears flowed freely. I would find the sheets wrapped so tightly around my fists that it was hard to untangle them from the nightmares.

When I opened my eyes, the wall was always there. It was so vast it covered the whole wall of my room. I imagined hundreds of tiny drawers filled with a lifetime of secrets. On nights filled with terror, the drawers would fly open uncontrollably. Open and shut. Open and shut. Open and shut. I had no control of them. The wall held the secrets of my life, and I would do anything to protect them. But I also knew that someday those drawers would have to be emptied in order for me to have any peace.

Not now, I'd tell myself on the worst of those nights. *Not tonight but someday, someday I will. Someday. That's my secret. I'm safe. I'm safe. I'm safe.*

My fingers circled the buttons on my pajama top as I repeat my soothing mantra.

Suddenly the locked door to my room burst open.

"Get up. Come on now. Get up, you're leaving," Jess said. Jess was one of the guards, and she didn't conceal her contempt for any of us. Her freshly starched and ironed sleeve scraped the side of my face as she shook me awake. Guards weren't supposed to touch us, but they did anyway.

"What are you talking about? It's not even morning," I replied. "What the hell is going on?"

Jess yanked me upright and flipped on the light. Bright florescent rays shocked my eyes wide open and reality surged through me like a train barreling along dark tracks.

"Leaving? What do you mean I'm leaving? Where am I going? Nobody said anything about transferring me." Had Shelly set me up? I remembered the red flag I felt when she first got there. Was I being transferred because of something I told Shelly in private? My mind was racing with possibilities.

"We know you and your friend Shelly are planning something. We're cutting you off at the pass. That's that," Jess said. "Now get up."

I stood up slowly, allowing the idea to sink in. It wasn't a dream because the cold cement floor felt like ice. And it wasn't Shelly, at least not directly. She didn't betray me; they were just upset because we were so close—couldn't have that.

The guard shined her flashlight directly into my eyes even though the bright fluorescent light was on.

"You awake in there? Anybody home? Get moving!" She laughed as she opened my locker.

They must be transferring me to Kingston, I thought. *Now that Shelly's here they're going to separate us, just because they can.*

"I want to see Shelly. Let me see her for just a minute," I pleaded.

"Nope. What do ya think we are, stupid?" she replied, handing me a paper bag to put my things in.

"You've been released. See you soon."

No parole hearing, no warning, nothing—I'd been set free.

House that I grew up in while in school

Age sixteen, just before heading to Yorkville, Toronto

Me at nineteen, just out of jail

"The Farm" in Northern Ontario

My adoptive parents on legal adoption day, two years old. Notice the blank stare and clenched fist (I still do that, thumb inside)

Confinement for a toddler

Me around three years old with my maternal
grandparents, just before leaving for Metz, France

Christmas and birthdays—never a happy occasion

Four years old posing in England

Rocky Mountains, Alberta, Canada, where I went to find the wild horses

The future is the past returning through another gate.
—Arnold H. Glasgow

Chapter 12

We Meet Again

Ten minutes later I was standing outside the prison gates, holding all of my possessions in a brown paper bag clasped tightly to my chest. The sun wasn't even awake. The entrance gate had become my departure gate, yet just as with my entrance, I didn't know where I was going once I passed through the arches. It was just a few days before Christmas and this was my gift: the bittersweet taste of sudden freedom. My legs trembled with uncertainty and my stomach filled with dread. I didn't want it to be like this. I wanted to turn around and run back in. But I knew they'd only send me away. They wouldn't even let me stay for Christmas.

Jess told me to wait there for the transport that would take me away. After several minutes of standing in the dark, the van pulled up beside me, and a door swung open.

"Get in. Haven't got all night," the driver ordered.

I looked behind me in case it was all a mistake and hoped to see the guards calling me to come back. But no one was there. There was nothing but empty, dark space behind me. It was not a mistake.

Heart Horse was trembling, as confused as I was. I climbed into the back seat wondering what would be next.

The gray-haired driver turned his head and winked.

"It's okay. You'll be fine," he said. "You look like a scared animal, honey, just relax. I'm taking you back to the city, that's all."

Something felt wrong. Twice they had refused me parole and then out of the blue I was on my way back to Toronto. Just when I was starting to feel like I belonged somewhere, I was told I didn't belong there—not even in prison.

The driver remained silent. I didn't mind; I was lost in my own thoughts anyway. When I looked up, the sky had become a light gray and the buildings were familiar. We were in downtown Toronto.

"I'll let you off at the corner, okay?" he said, pointing to the right.

"I guess," I answered, not really knowing any other option.

The van pulled over and eased to a stop at Dundas and Bay. Without a good-bye or a good luck, the driver sped off, leaving me standing in the snow with my brown paper bag and nowhere to go.

Shit. What now?

Looking around, I slowly took in the city's morning chaos. Every noise, every light, every honk seemed magnified a hundred times over. I'd been in an organized, sterile world for so long that this world that had once been so familiar had turned strange and overwhelming.

Inside my paper bag was a crisp white envelope. It held information that would dictate what I could and couldn't do for a while. I had to deliver it to the parole building first thing after they opened. The parole board would still be watching me for many months, making me show up regularly and tell them whatever it was they wanted to hear. No sense making them mad. I'd be there.

Daryl's number was waiting for me inside my journal. I wanted to call her, but it was too soon. I'd call her once I got settled somewhere.

But first I needed to get my things. I walked two or three miles to the house on Selby Street, tired, hungry, and eager to see Kenny and the guys and pick up my things. I couldn't wait to play my guitar. It had been too long, and now that Jay and Daryl had helped me find the music inside me once again, it was practically all I could think about.

But when I got there, I was dumbfounded at what I saw—or more accurately, what I didn't see. The house was gone.

What? That's not possible! How could an old Victorian funeral home simply disappear?

But it had. I asked around and learned it had been torn down. There was nothing left of it.

I headed east on Dundas Street, figuring I'd deliver my new life instructions to the parole office, when I decided to stop at Norm's Café, the coffee shop I liked to hang out at. I knew just about all my friends would be there.

They were. I asked about Kenny.

"Shit, man, Kenny split a long time ago," some guy said.

"Yeah, must've been over a year since I seen him," another said.

"Where'd he go?" I had to find Kenny—he had everything in the whole wide world I owned, including my guitar. I had to find him.

"I heard he OD'd," someone said.

"Had a stroke," another said.

"He's just gone. Too bad, too, Kenny always had good shit."

"Yeah, but Para-Dice Riders deal that shit, now; they got it covered. That what you lookin' for?"

What do you think, buddy? I said to Heart Horse. *Maybe a bit of Street Horse to settle our nerves?*

Heart Horse neighed and reared up on his hind legs but then fell silent.

A couple of weeks evaporated into thin air. I hung out at Norm's, where Street Horse pushed Heart Horse aside. In Chinatown, there was a bar called the Continental. I knew some of my friends from prison went there, so one night I decided to check it out.

I walked in and got a table. The air was thick with cigarette smoke and foul language and the wailing of Patsy Cline. My fingers occupied themselves playing with the saltshaker and drawing horses out of the wet rings left on the table from the twenty-five-cent draft someone had placed in front of me. Everyone was happy to see me, and they bombarded me with questions about those I'd left behind inside.

The place was loud with laughter. I wondered why I felt so sad; I was free. I didn't have to wake up at the crack of dawn to do as I was told. But I'd been so many places, found myself in so many different environments, and none of it ever felt right. I was a chameleon of my childhood home, learning to adapt to whatever mood my mother was in, to be whatever she wanted me to be—obedient servant, precocious pianist, invisible ghost—in order to survive. Now I'd become a chameleon of the streets.

Why is that? I don't belong here either. I can't trust these people. They really don't want me or love me. Where do I go now?

I had trusted so many people—people who had betrayed me, framed me, hurt me. Why didn't I see it coming? And when I did see it coming, why couldn't I protect myself? What was lacking in me, or contained inside me, that turned them one by one against me? Why was I so disposable?

Then again, when I did know enough to doubt, I got it all wrong. I saw red flags when Shelly came, but she befriended me, cared about me, never betrayed me. It was a good thing I had ignored those red flags. But what would I do the next time I saw red flags? Pay attention to them or ignore them? The demons of doubt weren't doing anything to protect me; they were only confusing me all the more.

If only Heart Horse could help me, comfort me with his love. But I hadn't seen him since Street Horse came back into our lives. Street Horse would settle my confusion; he always did.

Days have a way of slithering up the alleys of desperation in the city. I couldn't remember any of them once they disappeared. *If we can't recall our lives, have we lived them?* I wondered. I forgot my days as quickly as I lived them.

But through them all, Daryl's number burned quietly inside my pocket. I wanted very much to call, but I was too embarrassed to do it. Every time I thought to reach for the phone, I felt an overwhelming sense of shame. I had returned to the bowels of the city and the comforts of Street Horse almost the instant I'd gotten out of prison. How could I let Daryl see that? I didn't want to contaminate something so good with the stench of hopelessness that had surrounded me since my release.

It was turning to spring, and as the snow melted away, the dirt of the city was exposed for what it was. There was no color to be found beneath the deceptive white blanket of winter, just colorless grays and browns. My eyes and heart longed for the vibrant colors of nature, and as I walked through the dirty slush, I remembered that Allen Gardens was only a couple of blocks away, right smack dab in the middle of the sleaziest part of town. The park was the city planners' attempt to give downtown people a taste of the natural world, so it attracted a lot of people looking for a dose of nature in the middle of the day. I liked it because it gave me a small taste of nature and brought me solace, while others liked it for the freewheeling sex and drugs. I doubted that the city planners had had that in mind, but wherever street people could congregate for free, there would always be sex and drugs. Crocuses and daffodils were just an added bonus.

"Hey, Claire! Hey, over here."

I turned, expecting to see one of the Downtowners. At first I saw nothing. Then suddenly a bright red coat jumped out from behind a maple trunk. I was stunned and not quite sure if I should run or stay. Then I saw her face, and I was even more stunned.

It was Daryl.

Before I could say anything, she broke the stunned silence.

"When did you get here? How are you? Did you get my note? Are you okay? Can we talk? It's so good to see you!" Daryl's questions came tumbling out of her, one right after the other.

I was frozen into silence, trying to grasp that she was actually standing right in front of me, as if by magic. I collected my scrambled thoughts and tried to answer, but I couldn't think of a single word.

"Say something. Aren't you happy to see me?" she finally asked, her smile making it clear that she was genuinely happy to see me.

I was so shell-shocked, confused, and happy that I stuttered and stumbled over my words. "Of course! Just surprised. Of course, I'm happy to see you, Daryl, of course I am!"

"But when did you get out? Why didn't you call me?"

"Been out since Christmas. I'm okay, I guess. Yeah, I got your note, thanks. Good to see you too," I sputtered. I must have sounded like I was completely disinterested in seeing her, when the truth was that I was flabbergasted and overjoyed. But I was also embarrassed for her to see me. I knew I didn't look good; I knew I looked like I'd been back on the streets for a while, and that wasn't how I wanted her to see me.

"Is Jay with you?"

"No," Daryl answered. "Jay's on the road with his new band. They're doing really well, and they're already working on their second album."

"His band? But what about you?" I couldn't imagine why Jay wouldn't want Daryl in his band, considering how beautifully she played.

"I've got my hands full right now," she said, "with law school and other things. But you'll see him. He comes by regularly when he's in town."

"Oh, yeah, that would be great. Gee, Daryl, it's so cool to see you. I hope I see you again sometime." My words still weren't expressing the excitement I felt at running into her, but more my shame at her seeing me so obviously back on the streets. That wasn't how I wanted Darryl to know me.

She flipped her shiny black hair over her shoulder, revealing a collection of bracelets and dangling earrings that jingled softly.

"Come on," she said with a smile. "I just live down the street. Let's have some coffee."

I hesitated. If she realized I was back using Street Horse, I doubted she'd be asking me to go to her house.

"Oh, come on, are you all booked up?" She grabbed my hand and starting across Gerrard Street.

I let out a nervous laugh and let myself be led away.

The neighborhood we were in was fast becoming one of the Yuppie Communities. Up-and-coming young professionals were buying the old brownstone houses—once stately homes that had been converted into multiple units, neglected and overrun by the poor and the addicted—and were remodeling them into expensive homes.

"I can't believe you live in this neighborhood, Daryl," I said, not sure if I was impressed or disappointed. The people who lived in those homes sure weren't the kind of people I'd been hanging out with.

"I can't believe it either," she replied, shaking her head in good humor. "A friend of mine from law school owns the house with her husband. We think of ourselves as sort of a blend of people living independently together. How's that sound?"

"How many of you live here?" I asked.

"Well, let's see. There's my friend and her husband, who's a lawyer, a brilliant Chinese mathematician, and a sociology professor. But they aren't stuffy establishment types, you'll see. They're really cool. You're really going to like them."

Hmm, maybe, I thought, but I just couldn't see them being impressed with a junkie Daryl had met in prison then plucked off the street. As thrilled as I was to see Daryl, I couldn't shake the feeling that I was some sort of stray she was bringing home.

I knew I didn't belong there—the park yes, but not Ontario Street. Yet suddenly I was standing on a front step on Ontario Street, waiting for Daryl to unlock the door to a newly restored brick house. Considering I grew up in an even more spacious and prosperous home and my parents were prominent members of the community, it was ironic that I felt so awkward, but my life had changed profoundly in the few years since I'd run away. Still, there was a part of me, however dulled, that continued to live up to the Hitchon name. I might look like a drug addict in the eyes of others, but I'd known my social place since birth.

Ouch.

Since *shortly after* birth.

"Don't you ever forget you are a Hitchon! That means you'd better act appropriately at all times!" She was screeching with rage after the school had called about a smoking incident. She didn't really care what I did, but she was pretty upset if it made her look bad. "You have a reputation to live up to and don't you forget it. It's not too late to send you away you know. You must, must behave properly."

I didn't know why being a Hitchon was so important to her. I didn't care. Someday I would have my real name. Maybe not now, but someday. That's my secret.

"Come on in, make yourself at home," Daryl said, throwing her red coat over a velvet chair.

"You sure?" I asked her, feeling unsure of myself.

"Of course. Come on. I'll make the coffee." Daryl pulled me through the doorway.

Kaleidoscopic colors shimmered through stained glass windows, throwing a beautiful pattern on the wooden hallway floors. Noticing the gorgeous oriental rugs, I quickly took off my boots and glanced in the living room as I followed her down the hall.

The home was stunning, and I was amazed that Daryl lived in such a place. Just as we passed the open French doors leading to the living room, I stopped and stared in disbelief. There, in the corner, was a black baby grand piano, as shiny as a new pair of patent leather shoes.

"Like it? My parents gave it to me," Daryl said, watching my expression. She knew I would be impressed, that I'd know how special that piano was in ways most people wouldn't recognize.

"It's the most beautiful piano I've ever seen," I whispered in awe. I really wanted to touch it and sit on the bench, but I was too afraid to ask.

She laughed knowingly.

"You can play later; right now we need to catch up."

Sitting in the cozy kitchen, drinking gallons of hot coffee, felt so foreign yet so familiar. Conversation flowed easily between us, as it should with old friends.

Except she's not really an old friend, I thought. *We've never even had a proper conversation. Be careful or she'll hurt you.*

Yet the more comfortable I felt with Daryl, the more uncomfortable I became, afraid that such a wondrous moment wasn't going to last. And even if it did, even if Daryl genuinely wanted to be my friend, I knew we couldn't possibly be friends when we were living such opposite lives.

As I hammered myself with my doubts, our words continued going deeper. Emotions slowly surfaced. Our connection tightened. She told me that her family had something to do with the discovery of a famous household product, and she was financially comfortable, even owned a cabin in northern Ontario. She told me that she was one of the few Jewish families in town and that she and Jay, who was also Jewish, had met as children and bonded over their shared identities as outsiders. And she told me that her mother was very nasty to her, a cruel woman whose abuse had led her to leave home at an early age. It was as if we were cosmological sisters, destined to meet.

Do I tell her now? Will she kick me out? What should I do?

The thoughts kept popping into my head, waiting for just the right moment when I could interject, when I could pounce on a sliver of silence and confess my return to Street Horse. The more we shared of our hearts and lives, the more *not* telling her felt deceptive and wrong. But each time I thought I'd open my mouth and confess my shameful secret, I stopped myself. I couldn't bear her rejection. I wanted our conversation to continue, perfect and vibrant, for as long as possible.

But then, after some time of catching up and confiding, her mood shifted. She wasn't smiling, and a subtle shadow seemed to fall over her like a veil of tender pain.

"I have something serious to tell you," she said, her eyes turning shiny with tears.

"Me too," I replied, watching as the tears began their journey down her cheeks. I got up and got her some tissues since I didn't know what else to do. "Go ahead. You go first," I said, handing her a wad of tissue.

"Okay. Where do I start? I'll just tell you and then we can talk," she said, pausing to take a sip of her lukewarm coffee. A moment of quiet passed and then she shattered the silence. "I have breast cancer."

The words hung in the air, suspended by disbelief. I didn't know what to say.

Before I could muster a word, Daryl wailed, "I'm only twenty-four and I have fucking breast cancer! I have to have a fucking mastectomy!" She crumpled into a ball of pain, convulsing with sobs.

I reached over and grabbed her hand. How could my drug problems possibly matter after hearing that?

"Oh my God, Daryl! I'm so sorry!" I moved to her side and we clung to each other, our sobs like wounded spirits joining us in pain. After several close but crushing moments of holding and hugging each other and washing each other's faces with our salty tears, it was time to tell her.

"I have to tell you something, too. I... I'm doing drugs again," I said. I pushed my tears away and stared into her eyes, waiting for the rejection. Maybe if she rejected me, her pain would disappear from my life. If I didn't have to witness her pain, I didn't have to feel it with her.

Our eyes met through the tears and another connection was made.

"It's okay; we'll figure it out," she said, sniffling and squeezing my hand.

A barely perceptible tremor fluttered inside me. It was Heart Horse. He'd returned. But how long would he stay?

So now I must lie down where all the ladders start.
In the foul rag and bone shop of the heart.
—William B. Yeats

Chapter 13

Facing the Demons

Both Daryl and I were fighting to stay alive, only in different ways. Our hearts were breaking together, for each other as much as for ourselves. In a bizarre way, the two of us who were so different were exactly the same.

"Why don't you move in with us?" Daryl asked, not long after we'd resumed our friendship. "We have plenty of room here, and you'll thrive among all this creativity." But I wasn't so sure. I didn't really fit in with her roommates; they were very much establishment types, what Jay once called "the plastic people," who in my view measured their worth by their material success. Looking back on it, I don't think there was anything at all unlikable about them, but at the time, people living in beautiful homes and pursuing careers were alien to the counterculture we were living. I just didn't see myself fitting in.

Yet I could see that they'd created a family of sorts, and the thought of moving in with them filled me with as much excitement as fear. But I knew that I wasn't like any of them. They were professionals. I was a junkie.

"You know you are welcome here," Daryl said. "The choice is yours. But you need to know that I'm not the 'me' you're used to. Cancer has really changed me."

I didn't really understand what she meant, because from everything I saw, she was the same Daryl I had gotten to know in prison, the kind and generous spirit who filled our lives with music, encouragement, and kindness.

And the truth was my options were limited. I didn't have any proper place to crash; I had been crashing on the floor of a different friend or new acquaintance every night. Living with Daryl would probably offer me not just a nice home, but also the chance to get some help. Funny how someone with such serious problems as Daryl was facing—trying desperately to defeat the cancer that was eating away at her life—was the only hope I saw for myself. Could Daryl save me along with herself? Then again, that was asking an awful lot from her, and she sure had enough to deal with.

Somehow, Daryl seemed to sense my turmoil.

"For you, it's the world of addiction that has defined you," she said as she tried to persuade me to set my doubts aside and move in. "For me, it's the mystique, the mystique of a disease that no one really knows much about. The disease now defines me, but it's the mystique that motivates me. Together I think we're more powerful than we are individually. We can help each other grow."

"Yeah, but what if the only thing that grows is your cancer and my addiction?" I asked her, always ready to throw a bucket of dishwater on any hint of hope.

She looked into my eyes and smiled like a wise shaman, decades beyond her years.

"I have a favorite poet, William Butler Yeats," she said, "When Yeats was old he wrote a poem called *The Circus Animals' Desertion*. It's about starting where things end. He wrote about going through the joys, the disillusionment, and the boredom. And then he wrote"—Daryl closed her eyes, just the hint of a smile on her face, as she recited the lines she'd seared into her heart—"'So now I must lie down where all the ladders start—In the foul rag and bone shop of the heart.'"

"That's beautiful," I said, thinking that it could have been written of my very own soul, even though I didn't quite get what it meant.

"There's another line in there that might be more clear," she said, once again sensing my thoughts. "It goes, 'All things fall and are built again. And those that build them again are gay.' He means that those who rebuild what has been lost are filled with joy, that everything in life is in flux; everything breaks down and needs rebuilding. And that's where a kind of beautiful sensibility unfolds. That's where we'll find our souls."

Daryl's precision with words was intoxicating. She spoke like she wrote—in lyrics. I was still confused about what it really all meant; after all, these were only words and the reality for me was about scoring some drugs and not finding some beautiful sensibility. But to say no to such a possibility—the possibility that we might really find a way out of our own miseries—was unthinkable. Daryl had entered my life as if by magic, and I knew if I didn't follow her lead there'd be no more magic sent my way.

So I moved in.

I shared a tiny room in the basement of the house with a schizophrenic named John; he was the brother of one of the roommates who lived upstairs. All the proper people lived upstairs. John muttered to himself, dressed in layers of sweaters, and needed to be reminded to take a shower. Of course, that pretty much described most of the hippies and street people I knew, but John also conversed with light sockets, which pretty much set him apart from the mainstream.

It was the nicest home I'd lived in since I'd left my parents' home, but as familiar as I was with material comforts, I knew I didn't belong there. I felt like an imposter pretending to be one of them. I fought the urge to run daily. I desperately wanted to rejoin my friends at Norm's Café, which was just around the corner.

But I couldn't leave; Daryl needed me, and I needed her. Together we created mesmerizing music. Lyrics of pain and struggle flowed easily. The paper piles on top of the piano grew by the day, and so did our respect for each other—and for the battles we were fighting.

But it wasn't all melodies and music. Soon after I moved in, Daryl had her mastectomy.

"I want you there, with me, when I have the operation," she told me shortly before the operation was scheduled.

"Oh, Daryl, no, I'm the wrong person for that. Hospitals really upset me." I still couldn't shake the memory of waking in the hospital to find my mother leaning over my bed and whispering that she wanted me to die. I just wasn't ready to walk through the doors of any hospital, not even for Daryl.

"But I need you there, Claire. You can't abandon me," she pleaded. I knew she wanted me to go with her; and I knew I should be there. But I just couldn't face what was happening to her; it was too much for me to take in at the age of twenty. I had seen enough death at this point, but I just couldn't grasp that a friend of mine might be dying—not like that. Not Daryl. I just wanted to pretend it wasn't real.

"I'm not abandoning you, Daryl. I'll be here when you come home." And I was. Although I didn't go to the hospital for her mastectomy, when she got home from the hospital, I took care of her.

I fed her and bathed her and brushed her hair. I cleaned her incisions and changed her dressings and made sure she took her medication. She was healing beautifully and giving those cancer cells one hell of a fight.

As for how Daryl was taking it, she handled the loss of her breast with grace, but she didn't think much of the prosthesis. She hated wearing it, but after a few times of not wearing it, she realized that all people did was stare at her missing breast, so she began wearing it regularly. At the end of the day, she'd pull it out and toss it around like a game of catch, laughing wildly to ease the pain.

When it came time for the chemotherapy and the radiation, she got really sick. Her beautiful, curly hair began falling out by the fistful, and she couldn't keep any food down. She became skeletally thin and looked more like a Holocaust survivor than a cancer survivor.

As I grew more courageous, I started accompanying her to the hospital for her treatments, and when we got home in the evening, we spent the night playing music (when she had the energy) or reading to each other. But it was hard for her to concentrate, and her energy was so low.

"I withdrew from law school today," she told me one day, and then she sat down and cried.

"I'm sorry, Daryl. I know how much it means to you," I told her, "but don't worry; you'll go back as soon as you get better."

We both knew that would probably never happen.

But then it did.

"I have good news," the doctor told her after the chemotherapy and radiation treatments had finished. "Your cancer is in remission."

No more amazing and welcoming words had ever been spoken.

"But that's no guarantee you're cancer free. It's stopped spreading, but you aren't out of the woods yet. We don't want to take any chances, so we want to continue treating it with medication, but you don't need any more radiation or chemotherapy at this point."

In other words, it was great news and no news. We still didn't know if she'd get better, but at least we had hope.

"Why don't you take a vacation?" her doctor suggested. "You've earned it, and the rest is just what you need."

"That's a great idea," Daryl said. "I'm not sure where I'd go, but I'll think about it."

"I've already been thinking about it" her doctor said, "and I have a house in Fort Lauderdale. I'd be happy to give you the keys if you'd like to spend some time in Florida."

Daryl could charm anyone, so it probably shouldn't have been such a surprise that of all her cancer patients, Daryl's doctor would offer her the keys to her own house—but she did and we were thrilled! The snow was still knee-deep in Ontario, and the chance to head to Florida for an early spring vacation was exactly what we needed. So packing a suitcase of meds and some swimsuits, we hit the road.

But we'd be crossing the border, which meant I'd need my birth certificate or a passport. And that meant going back to Belleville.

And seeing my mother.

"She can't possibly be as bad as my mother," Daryl said. "Mine is absolutely evil!" Daryl had told me stories of her mother who, like mine, could be cold, abusive, and cruel. But Daryl had never been adopted, and although I knew birth mothers could be unloving and heartless, it was hard for me to fathom a birth mother who could be as cold and cruel as a mother who'd never bore, nor wanted, her child in the first place. But I knew Daryl was hurting from more than just her cancer; I knew she carried deep, undisclosed secrets from her own childhood that had scarred her deeply. She shared so much of herself that I didn't dare ask for more.

"I don't know, Daryl," I said, laughing uncomfortably. It was hard to mask the pain and dread I was feeling at the thought of encountering my mother again. "Mine makes no secret of how much she hates me."

"She doesn't hate you, Claire," she said, reassuringly. "If anything, she probably hates herself."

Well, maybe, I thought, *but what difference does it make? It's me she takes it out on.*

"All I know is that she isn't going to be happy to see us. But I can't wait to see the look on her face when we pull up!" I said, though deep down I knew I could wait a lifetime before seeing her face again. We laughed and swapped stories of our abusive, hateful mothers, howling in hysterics through the unspoken hurt and emptiness we both felt as we drove to the town I'd fled just a few years before.

Had it already been a few years? It was hard to believe, but I was already twenty years old with a prison record and a drug addiction, and now a best friend who might be dying. That was an awful lot to take in for someone so young, and an awful lot to conquer. I wasn't sure that I could do it.

"Daryl, I can't go through with this. Let's go back. I don't want to see that bitch ever again." The closer we got to Belleville, the more nervous I became. By the time we pulled into my old neighborhood, I was nauseated and trembling, my brain spinning with a thousand memories that I'd thought I'd locked away forever. But my nerves settled when I felt Heart Horse nervously galloping inside me. Even though he was as nervous as I was, just knowing he was there beside me comforted and calmed me. It was so rare to feel Heart Horse anymore; Street Horse had pretty much permanently taken his place. As we pulled into the drive, boy did I wish I had some Street Horse to take the edge of the visit I was about to endure.

"Wow, Claire, you never told me you grew up in such a place!" Daryl was clearly impressed by the large, brick Victorian house I'd lived in for so many years.

"Well I needed a few extra rooms to hide in!" I joked, just as my mother stepped onto the porch to see who'd pulled into her drive. As we got out of the car, the scowl on her face said it all.

"What are *you* doing here?" she asked, as if I were some mistress she'd told to get lost. I reddened with embarrassment and anger as my mother looked Daryl up and down, obviously disgusted by her thin frame and nearly bald head. She no doubt thought Daryl was one of my junkie friends.

"This is Daryl," I said, in a stone cold tone. "We're going to Florida. I came to get my birth certificate."

My mother stood silently, her face fixed in a frown, as if pondering how she could turn down the request in a way that would make me look insufferable for having the nerve to want proof of my own existence.

Fortunately, Daryl broke the silence.

"Hi, Mrs. Hitchon," she said with a huge smile as she extended her hand. "It's so nice to finally meet you. Claire's told me so much about you."

I resisted the urge to snicker.

"Hello," my mother replied in an excruciatingly polite tone that could freeze Lake Ontario. She limply shook Daryl's hand and turned back to me. "You'd better get in. I don't want the neighbors seeing you out here. They think you're dead." She said it so matter-of-factly like she'd just said, "They think you're away at college." Daryl looked at me, and we shared a knowing gaze as we passed through the door and into my mother's home.

Everything was just as I'd left it: impeccable and cold. I thought back to Russell's house and the birds and doilies that his mother had collected over the years, giving her home a warmth and personality that survived her long after she'd died. Here, where my mother still lived, such small but meaningful touches were completely absent. The stiff, chintz couch sat in the living room like a wide-hipped dowager holding court before the easy chairs, themselves so stiffly uncomfortable that no one dare sit on them for long. The piano that I'd practiced and played on throughout my childhood now looked like a highly polished piece of furniture, its only function to look beautiful. I wondered if its keys had even been touched since I'd left. I hoped my father was still playing.

"Oh! That's such a beautiful piano, Mrs. Hitchon!" Daryl walked over to it and lifted the polished lid to reveal the keys.

"Close it right now," my mother snapped, swiftly stepping up to the piano and closing the lid. "That's not a toy," she said, as if we were six years old.

"Mom, Daryl is a beautiful pianist; you should hear her play."

"You were a beautiful pianist once as well," she replied, "but our money was wasted on your lessons. I'll go get your birth certificate and you can be on your way."

"While you're looking, can you get my adoption papers as well?" I asked her. I figured I'd need them at some point in my life and didn't want to make a habit of returning any more frequently than I had to.

"Claire, this is certainly not the time to discuss that," my mother said. It was a wonder there weren't icicles hanging from the whiskers that covered her chin.

"Claire has a right to her legal papers," Daryl interjected, the law student in her coming to life. "They're her property."

My mother slowly turned her head toward Daryl and glared with anger I'd only seen moments before she attacked. If looks could kill, Daryl would have withered away in that instant. Although she didn't say a word, my mother's message was unmistakable: *You* are not a part of this family. *You* have no say in this matter. *You* should mind your own business.

I knew the feeling.

It was a surreal moment like something out of a movie. I had never had anyone speak up for me before, and I was horrified and thrilled at the same time. I wasn't sure what I should do. Up until that moment, I'd thought I'd understood how bad and wrong my life had been growing up with such a cruel, uncaring woman. But in that single moment, when Daryl, so much older and wiser than I, challenged my mother right before my eyes, I realized how twisted my life had been living in that house.

My mother let her glare linger just a moment longer then turned and left the room.

The instant her back had left our view, Daryl grabbed my arm and whispered into my ear, "You're right; she's a real bitch!" I felt a stab of perverse pride at being "right," and a pang of bitter pain at the cold, hard truth of who my adopted mother really was.

After some giggles, I showed Daryl around the house, passing through the many rooms adorned in ostentatious displays of privilege and unlived lives. My old room was the same as it was when I left— blank, cold, and bare like a showroom no one lived in. And there was my bed, in the same perfectly made chenille bedspread, its nubs all smoothed into the same direction, the crease under the pillow still razor sharp, the same gray blanked folded accordion style, and perfectly centered, exactly as I'd left it, to her specifications.

I'd always hated that bed and that room. Both came with an endless litany of rules that had to be followed precisely or all hell broke loose. I was never allowed to personalize it, to hang anything on the wall or display anything that didn't fit the décor my mother desired.

"What's that smell?" Daryl asked.

I sniffed a few times. "I don't know," I said. It smelled of curry and disinfectant, an utterly bewildering odor I couldn't possibly fathom.

"We rented out your room to a sheik," my mother's voice shrilly explained behind our heads. We turned and saw her standing in the doorway. She'd been following us, watching our every move.

"A sheik?" Daryl asked while I rolled my eyes.

"Yes, a sheik," my mother answered, her chin whiskers practically dripping with icicles from the chill in her voice. She didn't elaborate, and we didn't ask. "I had to clean the room twice after his departure last week."

Sterilized after the sheik's departure. It figured.

"We're fine, Mom; can you get me the documents?" I couldn't stand her hovering, but she didn't seem willing to budge.

"I think you two have been here long enough. It's not your room anymore, Claire; you should know that." With equally chilling glares, we left her standing in the bedroom, and I finished the house tour.

When we reached my dad's library, I saw his chair—the chair I would hide behind to get away from her, where I would trace my finger around and around the buttons on the back. It was the chair that protected me when my father could or would not.

Ever since I was little I had an ability to memorize objects, textures, and scenes by tracing with my fingertips on whatever surface was available to me.

My pointer finger finds the perfect spot on my daddy's chair, and I begin tracing the horse scene. The scene my uncle Willy told me about. Here are the mountains, around these buttons, and there is the forest, around those buttons. And here, right above these buttons, are the wild horses.

"Claire? Where are you, Claire? Get back in here this minute! I'm going to teach you a lesson you'll never forget, so you show yourself right now. Do you hear me, young lady?"

Her voice is mean and scary, but I don't care. My horses will be coming around these buttons any moment. Right, Heart Horse?

"And this is my dad's library," I said. "I love this room." The golden rays of the late afternoon sun glistened through the leaded glass windows, casting their light on the dusty leather spines of my great-grandfather's books. Somehow this room meant more to me than my own bedroom, because in this room was my wall of secrets.

"And see that library file over there," I said, pointing to a wall lined with heavy oak cabinet drawers that in some other lifetime had held Dewey Decimal cards.

"Beautiful antiques," Daryl said, looking around. But before I could say another word, we heard a car pull into the driveway. After straining to hear the whispered conversation in the foyer, I heard my father's footsteps approaching. Moments later, he stepped into the library.

"Well look who's here! Claire, why didn't you tell us you were coming down?" My father gave me a warm hug, and then turning to Daryl, he said, "You must be Claire's friend. How are you?" They introduced themselves and had just begun chatting when my mother returned with my birth certificate.

"Here," she said, thrusting it into my hand. I stared down at it and winced. It wasn't a real birth certificate; I'd never had one of those. This piece of paper was as fake as my mother. It said I had been born to her, but as she had made clear, that wasn't the case. It was a false documentation of a false birth, a signed, sealed, and delivered fabrication of how I'd come into this world and into her life.

"Where are the adoption papers?" I asked, looking up from the certificate of my fraudulent birth.

"I told you, Claire; this isn't the time," my mother repeated. My father visibly retreated, taking a step back before leaving the room altogether. But I couldn't blame him. He would have to listen to her bitter, venomous words long after we were gone. "Is there anything else you came for?" she asked, so eager to be rid of us it was a wonder she didn't just call the police straight away to have us forcibly removed.

"No, that's all. We have to get going," I said, not even bothering to look her in the face. I just wanted to get out of there. Daryl excused herself to go to the bathroom, and I was almost surprised my mother didn't intervene to keep her from sitting on her precious toilet. But the moment Daryl had stepped out of the room, my mother pounced.

"That girl is nothing but bad news," she hissed. "Just look at her; she's even worse off than you. You know you can't bring your junkie friends over here!"

"She's not a junkie," I hissed back. "She has cancer."

"Cancer my eye—that girl doesn't have cancer any more than I do. She needs one of those fixes."

"What do you know?" I snapped. "She's had a mastectomy and just finished chemo!" My mother paused, realizing I might be telling the truth. But that didn't stop her.

"She's only going to use you, Claire, like all your friends."

"You don't know anything about her," I said, "and she's a better person than all your friends combined!" I couldn't get out of there fast enough and wondered if going to Florida was even worth the trouble, considering it meant seeing her.

"One of these days you're going to find out that the only people who care about you are your own family, and not these stray druggy friends of yours that you pick up off the street. You'll find out soon enough that I'm the only one who'll ever care for you."

Every word and sentiment that came out of her felt like a slap in the face. But this ironic claim beat them all. To think that she would dare suggest that she'd ever cared for me in the first place was a joke; claiming no one would ever even come up to her pathetically low standard of caring for me was just another one of her put-downs intended to make me feel bad.

"Oh, please!" I groaned.

"And another thing," she added, just as Daryl returned, "this whole going to Florida notion of yours is ridiculous. You're only going to get yourselves in trouble and probably wind up in an American jail."

Man, was that woman a buzzkill.

"We aren't going to end up in any jail," Daryl said. "And we're going whether *you* like it or not." The nice, polite Jewish girl who entered the house was gone, and a pissed-off, "don't mess with me," fiery future lawyer was standing before us, bald head and all. Daryl wasn't taking any more of my mother's shit. That was something my mother wasn't used to.

Her face sputtered and spun before she fixed it in her infamous glare and declared, "I think you'd both better leave now."

Which is exactly what we did.

We are not meant to stay wounded.
By staying stuck in the power of our wounds,
we block our own transformation.
—Caroline Myss

Chapter 14

Crocodile Rock

"Don't worry," Daryl said as we drove off, "you don't have to see her ever again if you don't want to. You were right to run away from that house when you did. She's a vampire; she'd suck the life out of anything beautiful."

I knew Daryl was right; my mother did have the personality of a vampire. For all the embarrassment, hurt, and anger I felt as the house I'd grown up in disappeared behind us, I found a strange pleasure in knowing that someone else recognized my mother for the cold-hearted witch that she was. And I did find a perverse enjoyment in the irony that someone as obsessed with how things looked to outsiders, insisting that everything be so perfect and beautiful, actually drained the world of any beauty or perfection just by the bitterness of her own soul.

But most of all, I wished she'd never been my mother.

If she'd never adopted me, I would have had a much different life. Maybe a worse life, but I doubted that. It was hard to imagine a more loveless, lifeless home, and once I started thinking about the cruel fate that put me in her care, my angry thoughts gained momentum until all I wanted was to go for a fast gallop with Street Horse—anything to block out my thoughts and stop the pain.

But there was no chance of that. After a quick stop in Toronto to get some more medication for Daryl, we were back on the road, Daryl medicated into tranquility and wishing she didn't need to be, and me wishing to God I was. We made a comical pair, especially with Daryl, doped up and happy, behind the wheel, while I rested my head against the headrest and thought about my headache and my mother, two excruciating pains that I'd give anything to be rid of.

"Okay, here's the border," Daryl said, bringing me back to the moment. I realized I'd spent the last part of the drive in silence, thinking about that woman, wondering who my real mother was, where she was, and what she was doing at that very moment. Did she have any other children? Was there something wrong with her that she couldn't keep me? Had she been forced by her parents or some church to give me away? Why had she done it? Who was she?

But those thoughts had to wait. The car was slowing to a crawl as we waited in line to cross. My heart began to race.

"Daryl, let's turn back! I don't know what I was thinking. I've got a record; they're never going to let me in."

"Don't be ridiculous, Claire. We can't turn back now, and it's not like they have a list or anything. Just relax and you'll be fine. There's no reason not to let you cross. You aren't carrying, are you?"

"No, of course not," I said. "I wouldn't try to bring drugs across the border. I'd end up back in prison."

"Good. Then there's no reason they won't let us cross."

I hoped she was right. I really didn't know one way or the other if I could get into the United States, but for some reason I was certain they'd tell me I couldn't get in. I had become so accustomed to being told I didn't belong, that I'd practically convinced myself that I wouldn't even be wanted by a nation. But my parole was over, and there was no way for them to know I'd ever even been in prison. There were no computers back then, so it wasn't like they could just type in my name and have my whole history pop up on a screen. I was just being paranoid, and I knew I had to relax.

"Where are you going?" the border guard asked, peering into the car, his eyes scanning the back seat for any bulging blankets concealing mountains of drugs or some illegal person we were helping to smuggle into the States. But *I* was the illegal person, I felt, cloaked in an invisible blanket of shame that I feared they'd somehow uncover.

"We're going to Florida, officer," Daryl said politely.

"For what purpose?" he asked, still scanning the car, our faces, and our expressions.

"A vacation," she said.

"Where?"

"Florida."

"For how long?"

"Ten days."

"Where will you be staying?"

"In a house."

"Your ID," he ordered, and Daryl handed him her driver's license. He looked it over then handed it back and addressed me.

"And where are you from?"

"Toronto," I answered. "We're both Canadian." He kept staring, his eyes fixing on our breasts. For some reason he wasn't letting us through.

"What's in there?" he said, gesturing with his chin toward a duffle bag in the back seat. It was made from a Guatemalan weaving and screamed "hippie drug stash."

"My medication," Daryl answered honestly.

His brows lifted.

"Would you pull over there?" he said, indicating the line for the cars to be searched.

Shit.

"I don't understand, officer," Daryl said, the lawyer in her coming to the surface. "We haven't done anything wrong."

"Just pull over there," he instructed, clearly not willing to entertain any alternative. Daryl and I heaved heavy sighs and muttered some obscenities then did as he told. After a long wait, several officers and a dog came to the car and began searching every inch of it. I sure was glad I hadn't brought anything along with me; one joint and I'd be back in prison, and this time Daryl wouldn't be coming to visit and teach music—she'd be on the inside right beside me.

The guard who'd stopped and quizzed us yanked open Daryl's duffle bag and began rummaging through her medications.

"Looks like we've got something," he hollered to his colleagues, and they all swarmed around him, hovering and buzzing over the bag like they'd just busted the French Connection.

"I told you, those are my medicines," Daryl said, her voice firm if not angry.

"Medicines, huh?" the guard who'd found them snorted, "Looks like you're trying to bring a whole lot of narcotics into Michigan," he said. "You got some connection in Detroit you're supplying?"

"No! I have cancer. Here. I have a note from my doctor; we're going to her house in Fort Lauderdale." I didn't think I'd ever seen Daryl so angry. Her face had turned crimson as she searched through her purse, cursing and bitching until she found the note from her physician. She shoved it at the guard.

"Look, lady, anyone could have written a note like that. You're going to have to come up with a better story than that," he said, his ignorance and hostility written all over his face.

But that was all it took for Daryl to blow her top. Literally. In one quick movement, she pulled up her peasant blouse, reached into her bra and yanked out her prosthesis. Then she flung it straight in his face.

"There! Satisfied? I had my tit cut off; is that a good enough story for you?"

They let us through.

Twenty-some hours later, we reached Fort Lauderdale, hot, sticky, tired, hungry, thirsty, but most of all, relieved. After stopping a couple of times for directions and getting lost in a maze of cul-de-sacs and winding streets named after long-forgotten Spanish heroes, we passed through a pair of wrought-iron gates and drove down the drive of an elegant, Spanish-revival home with red-clay tiled roof and huge arched windows, impossibly tall palm trees sprouting from a perfectly groomed lawn.

"I think my doctor makes too much money," Daryl said, "if this is her second home."

"We might just never go back," I said as we wrestled with the key and stepped inside.

The house was filled with light and color and a sense of peace; it was just what we needed. There was a swimming pool and covered patio in the back; inside, the Mexican-tiled floors and whirling ceiling fans kept the house comfortably cool. We each nabbed a spacious bedroom, got into our swimsuits, and in minutes we were sitting by the aqua-colored pool sharing a pitcher of rum and pineapple juice, Jimmy Buffet singing from the boom box.

"Let's go dancing tonight!" I suggested as we mulled over all the things we wanted to do.

"I'd love to go dancing, Claire, but I just don't have the energy," Daryl said. "I'd just like to take it easy."

I knew she was right. She'd come there to rest and recover. I'd come to check out the beach scene and have some fun. But going out without Daryl didn't sound very fun at all. So that first night, we stayed in.

And the second.

By the third night, we were getting on each other's nerves. Daryl still wasn't feeling well, and even though the doctor had told her that her cancer cells were in remission, she didn't seem to be getting any better at all.

"I just want to feel better! I want to go to the beach and go dancing and party and have a good time, Claire, I really do," she explained. "But I feel so weak that it's taking everything I have just to sit by the pool and relax."

"I know, Daryl," I assured her, "I know." And I did know. I knew she was hurting and I knew she was weak, but I really wanted her to be better. I wanted us to have a normal vacation and do normal things, but then again, neither of us was normal.

And as sick as Daryl was, I was also feeling pretty shitty. I hadn't had any drugs for days, and I was getting restless and anxious and needed to get out of the house.

"You go," she said. "I'll be fine."

A couple of nights I did go out, but when I came stumbling back late at night, it was clear she wasn't fine with it. She never asked where I'd been or what I'd been doing, but one look at her face the next morning and I knew she didn't approve.

When Daryl finally felt up to it, we were able to take a little road trip to Key West.

"Come on, Daryl!" I called to her, hopping out of my jeans. I was wearing my swimsuit underneath my clothes and couldn't wait to get into the water. "Let's dive into the water just as the sun begins to set. I want to swim straight to the setting sun! Come on!"

Daryl laughed but didn't budge.

"You go," she said. "I'll watch you. I'm not feeling well."

It had gotten so that I'd heard that so many times. I never knew if she really meant it, or if she was just saying it so she didn't have to join me. I shrugged, said my prayers to the sun, and dove into the waves coming straight at me. The moment I hit the water I felt buoyant and alive like a playful dolphin thrilled to be home. But then, in an instant, a wave caught my belly and washed me right back to shore, belly surfing face-first right into the gravelly sand, practically scraping my face off.

After picking out the gravel that had embedded in my cheeks, we drove through the Everglades to the tune of Elton John's song *Crocodile Rock*, rocking and singing and having a great time. Then we got a flat tire. It was dark and the moss hung from the trees like giant cobwebs; we could hear all kinds of animals waking up, and we knew we were surrounded by alligators and snakes and didn't dare get out of the car. It was so creepy and we had no way out. We didn't have a spare, the car was filled with Daryl's drugs, and I looked like I'd just been beat up by an electric sander. There were no cell phones back then, and we had no idea who would save us, so we locked ourselves in the car and waited.

"I told you we never should have come out here," one of us said.

"If you hadn't slept so long, we could have been on the road earlier and at least it wouldn't be dark," another one of us said.

"Don't blame me!" we both said.

After hours of bickering and being startled by every sudden sound or scary noise, someone finally came along and towed us into town.

"Let's go home," Daryl said.

And at last, we agreed.

You must declare who you are in public.
Public declaration is the highest form of visioning.
—Neale Donald Walsh

Chapter 15

My Soul Is Not for Sale

"Have you thought about getting a job?" Daryl said to me one day. I thought it would be a good idea, too, actually. I'd even gone to a few different dry-cleaning places, but as soon as they learned I'd gotten my experience in prison, that was the end of that conversation. Or they were willing to overlook it in exchange for some "favors." After half a dozen of these encounters, I pretty much gave up.

"I know I need a job, Daryl, but no one's going to hire me. You know that."

"No, I don't know that at all, Claire. I think someone will hire you. You're really bright and talented. You just need to look harder."

Instead, I'd head to Norm's. Norm's was my home away from home, my comfort, a place I could go and get away from the yuppies, the Plastic People. They were nice enough, but it was pretty clear that Daryl's roommates wanted me out. The questions about my past, about my future, about my present, all added up to, "What are you doing here and how soon before you're gone?" But no one ever came right out and said anything to me.

But they said it to Daryl; I could tell.

"Daryl, I think I should probably get my own place," I told her, hating the thought of leaving but knowing it was for the best. Still, my life had seemed to blossom musically since moving in with Daryl. Since returning from Florida, we stayed up till all hours writing and playing music, and every once in a while, when Jay was in town, we'd head over to his place and do some recording. The music was pouring out of us. We were writing lyrics like poetry slams, each perfect syllable and word was precise and powerful, with sheets of music and scribbled songs strewn all around the floor beside the piano or piled high on top of it. It was an amazing experience and the most creative period of my life, so I didn't want to just walk away.

But I knew I didn't belong there.

"What you need to do, Claire, is stop going to Norm's. You're only going to get sicker if you keep going there. You know that. You say you want to get straight, but I know as soon as I go to sleep, you're heading over there."

"You know, Daryl, the last thing I need right now is for you to judge me," I said, feeling more defensive the closer she got to the truth of the matter. I did need to stop going, but that seemed impossible as long as I lived with the yuppies. I felt so out of place in that house with all those professional types, and Norm's was about two blocks away. It was pretty much like having a heroin dispenser in the backyard.

"I'm not judging you," she said tenderly. "It's just that now that I'm getting better, I want you to get better too."

"I am better, Daryl," I said. "Don't worry. I just go there to see my friends, is all."

Of course, I still worried about Daryl. She was better than she'd been in a long time, but her energy was still very low and she still had her bad days. Her doctors were confident, however, that things were looking good. And I still needed to spend time with Street Horse to know that, no matter what happened, at the end of the day Street Horse would be waiting to comfort and hold me tight.

"But we're your friends, here, Claire," she said, to which I just gave her a look. "I know you feel like you don't fit in here," she went on, "but they're just concerned, that's all. If you'd stop going to Norm's, I think you'd discover that you have a lot more in common with the people here than you realize."

I genuinely wanted to believe that my identity was more than just being a junkie, and at first I'd thought that being around all these successful people might be good for me. But instead, it only seemed to emphasize how different I was from them—which sent me right straight to Norm's and the Continental, where I felt I had a sort of second family, imperfect and flawed as they were.

But Daryl was right. I had to stop going on these nightly tours. I just didn't know how.

"Hey, baby, how about coming home with me?" I looked him up and down and turned back to my near-empty beer.

"Go on, get outta here!" one of the butches told him, stepping between us, her hefty body blocking me from his view. "She's not available." With a glum look the John slunk away and the leather-clad butch bought me another beer.

"The longer you keep coming here without going home with anyone, the more they all want you," she said, grabbing a chair, spinning it around, and swinging her leg over it like a dude. She sat across from me, straddling the chair turned backward, its back like a shield she clung to. It seemed one horny letch had been replaced by another as she fixed her admiringly eyes on mine.

"Not interested," I said, taking a swig of the cheap sudsy beer. She waited another moment, and when no smile came her way, she shrugged and walked away.

I may have been scowling on the outside, but the truth was that I was impressed that all these old husky lesbians were so hot for me. I'd started coming to the Continental for the twenty-five-cent drafts but stayed for the dykes and the queers, who had become my friends. They were misfits, like me, and didn't hassle me as much as the guys. If I said no, they left me alone, but for the most part, they took me under their wing. And the drugs were as plentiful as at Norm's.

I really liked the women at the Continental; they reminded me of the bikers I used to hang out with. The biker world had changed since I'd gotten out of prison. Organized crime had eventually taken over their drug networks, and once that happened, things started getting violent and ugly. Ever since Kenny split, the entire vibe had changed. So I stayed away, and the old butch broads at the Continental took their place.

It was one of the roughest gay bars downtown, right in the middle of Chinatown and a notorious area for gambling, drugs, and hookers. Some of the group turned tricks across the street in a tiny hotel run by a Chinese couple that watched out for anything unusual. They liked me there; I may have been considered just another street kid elsewhere, but to the rough-talking, leather jackets with their big muscles and slicked-back hair, I was elegant and attractive, one of the fems. I just didn't turn tricks, and I didn't go home with anyone.

It was my first real exposure to the gay world, and I seemed to fit right in, even more than at Norm's. I was flattered by the attention and comforted by the privacy. They might have shown interest, but no one messed with me. Of course, just as the butch had said, the longer I kept to myself, the more untouchable—and desired—I was. It was the perfect place to get away from a house full of plastic people.

"Hey, you wanna make some easy cash?" It was one of the girls from Norm's. I didn't know her well but had seen her around, hustling.

"No," I said, shaking my head. "If I could, I would, but I just don't think I could pull it off." I smiled, showing her that I wasn't being judgmental. I just didn't have it in me to turn tricks, no matter how broke I was. It was as if no matter how far I had fallen, there was still some small part of me that was determined to live up to the Hitchon name, to prove to myself that I did belong in my family.

But without dealing anymore, money was tight. Maybe it was worth a try.

"Come on, you can do it!" she said, "Just come with me and I'll show you."

"No, thanks; these guys are so dirty and greasy and filthy. I just can't imagine doing that."

"Not the Asian guys," she assured me, "they're real clean and they wash up. You gotta wash up for them too—make sure all your parts are clean. They're not dirty at all."

Hmmm. Well, maybe, I thought, but my heart just wasn't into it.

"Come on!" she said one last time, practically dragging me out the door. Before I knew it, we were a couple of blocks down the street and she was flirting with a couple of young guys in their late teens or early twenties—my age. Next thing I knew, we were all heading off to a dingy hotel on Jarvis street.

"I don't think I can do this," I said to my friend while the guys went to buy some wine.

"Claire, you can't back out now," she said, beginning to get irritated. "You said you'd come along, so now that's what you're doing. You wanna make some fast cash, don'tcha?"

"I guess," I said, not knowing what else to say or do. Just then the guys came back from the liquor store with a bag full of wine and chips, and we went around the corner to an old run-down building. The guys paid some cash at the front desk, and we climbed some dark stairs to a tiny room that reeked of sex and old cigarettes. The bed wasn't even made; the sheets were just pulled up, barely concealing the evidence of the previous users' activity. We cracked open a bottle and sat down.

We partied all night, but that was all. Some drinking, some drugging, and a lot of laughing, and then we passed out. By the time we woke up on the floor the next morning and headed home, I could tell my friend was pretty upset, since we didn't make any money.

After that I knew I wasn't cut out for that kind of life.

I started drinking pretty heavily once I started hanging out at the Continental. The drinks were only a quarter, and people were always buying me rounds. The tables were no bigger than barstools, and it wasn't be long before they'd be covered with beer glasses and half-empty pitchers and the fights would start breaking out.

Most of the fights were over nothing at all, and the rest were over next to nothing. Even the accidents were cause for a battle. Inevitably someone would stumble into a table and send everything flying, the crowd erupting in cheers and jeers. Half the time someone got blamed for shoving somebody into the table, and next thing you knew they were being slammed into the next beer-covered table like a barroom brawl on some old Spaghetti Western.

One day I was the one who got slammed.

I don't remember how the fight got started or what it was all about, but before anyone intervened, I ended up with a throbbing shiner.

"I need some ice," I said, leaning back on my chair and holding an icy glass of beer to my cheek.

"Hang on," someone said, "we'll fix you up." A couple of girls took off to get something in Chinatown, and I ordered another beer. Before I could finish it, they were back, carrying a plastic container.

"Here, have a beer," someone said, pouring me another.

"Close your eyes," someone else said, and I dutifully complied, waiting for whatever stinky ointment they'd gotten from the Chinese medicine sellers. Fermented snake oil or some such thing, I figured.

I felt something cold and wet placed right beneath my eye, followed by another and another. I opened my eye a crack and let out a scream. They were placing dark, slimy things on my face, holding them in place with their fingers until they attached themselves to my flesh. And when they did, I felt them move.

"What the hell!?" I screamed, struggling to sit up. I felt a pair of hands push me back into my seat, and more of the things were being put on my face. Now I could feel them crawling across my eyes and my cheeks. I opened my eyes and saw dark blotches squirming and growing, getting bigger and bigger until they became the size of giant sausages bigger than my own nose.

They were leeches. And they weren't just crawling around my eye, they were sucking my blood. Then they started falling off. One by one, fat from my blood, they fell onto the table, my shoulders, my hair, and the floor.

"All right, now go to bathroom and look in the mirror," someone said. I got up, made sure there were no leeches in my hair, and went straight to the bathroom. There in the mirror was my eye, red but barely swollen. It would be fine in the morning, a bit bruised but nothing like I'd expected. The leeches might have been disgusting, but they had worked.

It reminded me of when I was little and ordered some plenary worms from a scientific company. They were tiny little worms the size of a pin, and if you cut off their heads, they'd just grow a new one. If you split their heads in two, they grew two heads.

I wanted to be a doctor back then, so I did all kinds of experiments on the plenary worms. I'd go to science fairs and wander in amazement at the science exhibits and experiments. I'd practically forgotten all about those years and those dreams, until that night at the Continental with the leeches sucking my face. Even though I was disgusted at first, they fascinated me; it was as though I was conducting a biology experiment on my very own face. And after a few beers, it didn't even matter.

"Claire, this has to stop," Daryl said, dabbing my eye with some makeup. "My roommates are really getting on me about you, and I'm going to have to make a choice between you or the house."

"That's all right, Daryl," I said. "I'll find a place. Don't worry about me."

"I do worry about you, and I'm not choosing the house over you. We can get an apartment together. I'm not as sick as I was, but I'm still recovering and I need your help. And besides, someone needs to keep an eye on you before you're completely out of control." Daryl finished her patch job with a dusting of powder, and my face looked practically normal.

"Good work, Daryl! You're a real artist!" I gave her a hug and said, "Okay, I'll think about it. But I don't want you making a lot of sacrifices for me."

"I'm making those sacrifices for *me*," she said, "and if you really want to split and live on your own, I won't stop you. But I think getting our own place will solve a lot of problems."

"All right, Daryl," I promised. "I'll think about it."

"Good," she said. "That's all I'm asking. That and stop getting in fights; the next one might not be as pretty."

"I'm not worried," I told her, "just as long as I have a steady supply of leeches on hand. Those things are amazing!"

"Let's hope it doesn't get to that," she said. Then we went into the living room, sat down at the piano, and sang songs about love and a world gone bad.

A few days later we found a big, sunny apartment not too far away, but fortunately, it was a bit further away from Norm's and the Continental. Maybe Daryl was right. Maybe I did need someone to keep an eye on me. I just wasn't sure if it would make any difference once night came along and Daryl was fast asleep.

Could I stay home and drink hot cocoa, or would I find myself right back at the Continental? I just didn't know.

Everyone is a moon, and has a dark side which
He never shows to anybody.
—*Mark Twain*

Chapter 16

Darkness and Destiny

A few months after settling into our new apartment, I found my answer. I bought a new guitar at a pawnshop and started to play. Our music filled the spacious rooms all day and all night, with Daryl at the keyboards and me on the guitar or vice versa. The music inside me kept pouring out, and although I continued to sneak out to Norm's and the Continental, the pull to stay home and make music proved a strong contender for my attentions.

For the first time in my life, it seemed there was something besides heroin that made me feel good. And for the first time in my life, I felt happy to be at home. I began to feel like I might really have a future making music, somehow, someway, if only I didn't screw it up by sneaking out one too many nights for a wild ride with Street Horse.

"I have an idea," Daryl said one day when we were musing about the approaching summer.

"What?" I asked, expecting her to suggest we do some busking in Yorkville. We'd talked about making money by playing on the streets, and that's where a lot of people were discovered.

"Let's take a trip up north," she said.

"Where?" I asked her. "There's nothing up there but wilderness and grizzly bears."

"We can go to my farm and fix it up," she said. "We can turn it into a music studio.

Now that was a curious idea. Daryl had mentioned she had some land in northern Ontario that she'd inherited. She called it "The Farm," but she'd described it as just some acreage and some dilapidated buildings, a place she might retire to someday.

"But I thought there was nothing there," I said. "Just an old run-down barn."

"There's an old farmhouse that we can fix up and a cabin. It's not much, but if we work hard, we can get it into good shape."

The idea was appealing, and we soon found ourselves talking about it all the time. The Farm became our vision of a music studio where people from all over Canada and the States could come and play music twenty-four hours a day, maybe even do some recording if Jay would bring his sound equipment up there.

The more we talked about it, the more real it became, until finally, as soon as the snow began to melt and we knew the roads would be clear, we were throwing all our tools, food, blankets, and musical instruments into the car. Then we drove into the wild for the next five hours, singing along to Neil Young: "There is a town in north Ontario..."

We were halfway to the North Pole by the time we reached The Farm. It was deep in the backwoods, alongside a lake, and off an unmarked dirt road that seemed to go on forever. "The Farm," I saw as we reached the end of the dirt road, was a couple of dilapidated buildings buried in decades of overgrowth and neglect.

"I guess it's going to need some work," Daryl conceded, laughing at the state of decay her property had been reduced to.

We parked beside the barn and got out of the car. I inhaled deeply, smelling the sweet scent of grass and wet earth, listening to a harmony of birds, insects, and distant animals calling to each other in a language only they could fully comprehend.

"Daryl, it's beautiful!" I said. It didn't matter that the buildings were falling apart; what mattered was that we had made it, that neither of us had died, and we were instead standing there, side by side, enveloped by nothing but peace and quiet. I looked over to Daryl and saw her face had become as serene as an angel. She was right where she needed to be.

"Come on, we'd better get this stuff into the house," Daryl said, opening up the trunk to the car. "The sun will be setting soon, and we have a lot of work ahead of us."

I jumped right in, not wanting to waste any time. There was no electricity or running water in the house, so we'd have to get settled in before it was too dark to do so. There was a lot to bring into the house, but it was a good thing we'd brought along plenty of food and wine, because once we were up there, I realized just how remote it really was.

The house was almost empty, except for an upright piano covered in a thick layer of dust and a few pieces of furniture: a beautiful, round antique table, with intricate carvings; an old velvet sofa; and a few chairs. Upstairs was a loft bedroom, and downstairs, through a pair of French doors opening to the living room, was another bedroom. Daryl claimed the lower bedroom, and I took the loft. When we got everything unpacked, Daryl made us a dinner of cheese, fruit, bread, and red wine, while I made a fire in the woodstove, lit some candles, and started dusting off the piano.

For the next few weeks, we lived with only nature and music—no drugs, no bars, no cancer treatments. We cleared brush, chopped wood, washed windows, scraped paint, repainted, hacked weeds, made repairs, hauled water, and cooked our meals on the woodstove like a couple of pioneer women. At night we sang and played by the light of a propane lamp and fell asleep by the fire, waking again at dawn. Life soon took on a new meaning and was becoming more than I could have ever imagined. And Daryl was, at long last, coming alive, her eyes sparkling once again as she dreamed of the future.

During the days we would make the trip a few miles down the road where there was a tiny lake. It was so beautiful and isolated, not a single cabin in sight. On good days we played catch with Daryl's prosthetic breasts and laughed. On bad days, when she still wasn't feeling fully recovered—or when my own body was feeling battered from not having any Street Horse—we just floated silently on the water, listening to the birds. On those days, if I listened carefully, I could feel the gentle nudging of Heart Horse trying to get my attention.

As I listened to the gentle wind pass through the trees and the birds singing their songs to each other, my mind turned to the Rocky Mountains and the words of my Uncle Willy, spoken so many years before. I imagined cool water lapping the sides of my bare skin, and I saw a diamond lake with all of its jewels. I thought of the wild horses Uncle Willy told me about and wondered when and where I'd one day find a horse of my own.

When night came, we pushed logs lined with candles into the lake, drank peach brandy, and talked of life and death and the connection between the two.

I was safe. I belonged there, in nature with the lake, far away from city life.

Life was good.

We stayed there a couple of weeks before returning to Toronto, but over the next few months we drove to The Farm every chance we got. Little by little it began to transform from an abandoned and dilapidated old farmhouse to a lovely, peaceful sanctuary. Soon we were inviting friends to come visit, and everyone who came brought an instrument, if they could play, turning the once-abandoned property into a musical oasis. Before long the possibility of turning The Farm into a music studio didn't seem like such a crazy idea after all; we only had to make it happen. But there was just one problem: Daryl wasn't getting better.

And neither was I.

As healing as The Farm had been, once back in the city, I was right back to sneaking out to Norm's or the Continental. Each time I thought Daryl never knew. But each time I came home, I'd find a note from her asking me to stop.

We never spoke about it. Her pain was killing me. And my pain was killing her.

"It's back," she said, one evening, after I'd returned from a day spent downtown that she knew better than to ask about.

And I knew better than to ask about *what* was back. Her devastated face told me all I needed to know: the cancer was back.

"Oh my God, Daryl, I… I… I'm so sorry!" I hugged and held her, and we cried in each other's arms before she explained.

"The doctor called me yesterday and asked me to come in. I didn't want to tell you, because I was hoping it wasn't as bad as it is. But it is. I'm going to die."

"Daryl, you don't know that; you can't be sure," I protested. Daryl couldn't die, wouldn't die. She'd been doing so well. What had happened?

"No, Claire, I'm sure. The doctor's sure. He's told me to get my affairs in order."

Get her affairs in order—what a cold, clinical way to tell someone to get ready to die.

That night would be my last trip to the Continental, I decided then and there. Daryl needed me, and she needed me to be healthy—just one last time. That would be it. That night, it would all be over. At last.

The Continental Bar was closing just as the morning was opening. I'd pulled out all the stops that night. I celebrated my final night at the Continental, my final night with Street Horse, drinking and drugging and dancing all night long. And with the first hint that the sun would soon rise, I said good-bye to Street Horse and all my friends from the bar.

Stepping out onto the street, a thick hairy arm grabbed my shoulder, jerking me back.

"Want to talk a bit? Come with me, no fuss, no muss," he said, flexing his biceps as he gripped me tighter.

I knew who he was. I didn't even have to look at him to know that voice. His grip intensified as he pulled me toward the parking lot. He wore the uniform of the Downtowners but he had the face of a cop, a very well-known cop.

He was known to take people off in his unmarked car, only to return them later, battered and bloody with a court date stamped on a yellow piece of paper stuffed in their back pocket. He was notorious for his violence and vengeance, and nobody wanted to cross paths with him. Behind his badge, he was an outlaw of the very worst kind.

"What do you think you're doing?" I screamed, pushing him off. "Get your bloody hands off of me!" I thought if I screamed at him loud enough, people would come. But no one came, and my cries went unheard. Everyone was still inside the bar saying goodnight, and the music was still playing, drowning out everything.

"Shut up. Get in," he grunted as he pushed me into the back seat of his infamous unmarked car.

"Let me out, *you pig*," I yelled. I kicked the door as he sped out of the parking lot up Dundas Street and into the dark.

"I've been waiting a long time to get you alone," he said. He lit a cigarette and looked into the mirror. "Yup, a very long time, and I can't wait."

I'd like to wipe that smile off of his face. Don't do it. Don't do it. Don't do it. Stay calm. Stay calm. Stay calm. Street Horse fled from my veins, and I felt the trembling fear of Heart Horse stirring inside me.

I watched his eyes in the rearview mirror as I felt around my jacket pocket for my horse knife, before remembering it was gone—gone with all my things that Kenny had promised to safeguard.

Dad and I are in the boat fishing.

"Here," he says. "Cut the line with this." I saw back and forth until the line snaps. "You can keep it but don't tell your mom!"

I wipe the knife off and hold it tightly in my fist in marvel. I don't get many presents. This is really special. I will carry my horse knife. Always. I will never let it go. This is my secret.

I looked at the cop and saw his eyes were dark and bottomless pools of pure hatred.

"Don't bother trying that with me," he said. "I know what you're up to."

The cold glimmer of a steel gun barrel appeared in the mirror.

He might really kill me, and no one would ever know, I thought. *And he knows that as well as I do.*

The dark streets flew by as he drove toward the lake. Soon the sun would be up, but it was too early for most people to be out, the streets still blanketed in gray. I had a good idea where we were going: Cherry Beach. It was well known as the place you didn't want to go to.

He jerked to the left and slammed on the brakes. I braced myself. *If I time it right, maybe I can run. Careful. Careful. Careful.*

As the back door swung open, I quickly threw my legs out and pushed off of the door. But in an instant, before I could take even a step, he grabbed a handful of my long hair and wrapped his hand around it, pulling it like a leash toward him.

Most days, Mother does my hair in braids. She always says I have enough hair for a dozen people. When she brushes it, she pulls so hard it makes me cry. I always ask her to stop. She never does. Then she pulls it so tight my face feels stretched like elastic. When she isn't looking, I put my fingers inside the twists and wiggle them around to make it looser. I can't make it messy of course, cause then she would know. That's my secret.

"Come on, you little bitch. Don't fight me. You know better than that. You get what you deserve with me," Spit flew out of his mouth as he talked. His face was the color of beets as we battled for control.

"You bastard," I yelled. "Let me go." I managed to get in one good kick before he struck back.

He wrapped his hand around my hair several times until his fist was close to my scalp then he pulled hard. I stumbled on some rocks, his grip tightening as he dragged me to the beach. Out of the corner of my eye I saw his free hand coming toward me. I closed my eyes and tried to duck, but his grip on my hair held me tight. His fist slammed into my cheek with a crunch. Immediately, my mouth filled with blood and my spit flew through the air and landed on his shirt.

"You asked for it, bitch," he said. "Don't say I didn't warn you."

He pulled me toward him, and we both lost our balance, falling onto the sand with a thud. He fell onto me, one hand still in my hair and the other fumbling for buttons and zippers. His breath was heavy with smoky hatred and lust. The last thing I remembered was the taste of damp sand mixed with blood and tears.

Where the hell am I?

I strained to open my eyes. One eye wouldn't open. I looked around with the good eye. My head was resting on a green bag that smelled like old, rotted pig feed, and one of my arms was wedged beneath it. I could hear cars and people, but I couldn't see them. Straight ahead I saw a concrete wall with huge, orange graffiti spelling the word, "Peace."

I tried to move, but the pain was unbearable. As I pulled my arm out from under the heavy green bag I struggled to focus. I was surrounded by garbage. I was in an alleyway with boxes, bins, and piles of trash. My fingers were swollen and bent at angles that shouldn't be. My jacket was gone, and my shirt was bloody and ripped along the sides.

I checked my lips with my swollen tongue. Pain shot up the side of my face as I tried to open my mouth. I felt my top lip and realized with horror that it was so swollen it had molded itself into the space under my nostrils. Both lips were cracked open and thick with dried blood.

I slowly tested my body parts, and despite the pain that shot through me with every movement, I didn't think anything was broken. The skin on my face and neck was torn like tissue paper, revealing patches of raw meat that oozed blood. I wiggled myself upright until I was sitting, my back against the garbage bags.

What the hell happened? How did I get here? How long have I been here?

This would be another secret to go into the drawers of the Wall. *Who can I tell? Who cares? If I tell Darryl, she will only become upset. She doesn't need this now. I'll be okay. I'll be okay. I'll be okay.*

Daryl said I'd been gone for two days. She wanted me to go to the hospital and have the rape kit done so it could be reported to the police. I laughed to myself, knowing it was one of them that did it.

"I'll be fine," I said reassuringly. "There's no need for any fuss. The bruises will fade." But I knew the memories wouldn't. Not for a long time.

"Claire, whoever did this is really dangerous. You need to report it."

"I can't, Daryl," I said. "It's not worth it."

She was disappointed in me for not fighting. I was disappointed in her for not getting it. We stopped speaking of it.

I hid in my room for two weeks, coming out only to go to the bars. Somehow my decision to end that life had ended on Cherry Beach.

"Claire, you have to stop this. You have to come out of your room. And you have to stop going to those bars. You are killing yourself." Daryl was sitting at the piano, playing scraps of lovely melodies, each one breaking off into thin air, disappearing into a sky full of silence.

"I just can't do it, Daryl," I told her. "I won't ever be like you and your friends. Everybody you know is so together, and you're so calm while you're body is being eaten up by the cancer. I'm nothing like that. I can't ever get to normal, because I don't know what that is. And I can't keep pretending that I'm already there, because I know I'll never get there."

Daryl's mouth tightened and her eyes narrowed. I knew I had disappointed her. She wanted me to be a brilliant musician and live happily ever after. She wanted me to help her cure her cancer. And she wanted me to get off Street Horse once and for all. None of those dreams of hers were possible for me—none of them.

"Claire," she said, clearly tense and tired, but still with a tenderness in her voice that came from her genuine, loving kindness, "for a while, I thought like you. I'd tell myself, 'I can't do it because I have cancer. I can't do it because I've been through so much. I can't do it because I might die.'"

"Well, yeah," I said. "You get it. You know exactly how I feel."

"No, I know exactly how *I* feel, and how I've felt. But when we start thinking like that, what is left?" She looked up at me, her fingers that had been melodically tapping the piano keys stopped and fell to her lap.

"Nothing but shit," I said, the cynical truth of my life having been hammered into me for as long as I'd been breathing.

"No, Claire, you can choose to believe that, but I won't, not anymore. I don't have enough time to wallow in that kind of negativity. I have no choice but to keep fighting."

"Look, don't talk to me about fighting; I've been fighting all my life!" I was beginning to get angry, though I knew my rising anger had far more to do with my own failings than they did Daryl's. She was remaining calm and thinking clearly, while I wanted to bolt to Norm's Café or the Continental and take Street Horse for a ride.

"Then *start* fighting, Claire," she said. "Start fighting for your life." She closed the lid to the piano's keys and turned on the bench to leave.

"And just where do I start?" I wailed. "Where? How? If you have all the answers, tell me how to do it!" I just wanted to fly out the door and never come back, to just get out of a world filled with pain and never return to it. That's what I'd do at any moment.

"I can't tell you how you can start; I can only tell you what I've had to do. I start by stopping. I start at the beginning, square one, doing something I love and telling one person I love very much that I want to grow up again. I'm fed up with myself."

Her words baffled me. How could someone as sophisticated, wise, beautiful, and talented as Daryl possibly be fed up with herself? And after all she'd been through.

"How can you be fed up with yourself?" I asked her. "I'd give anything to be like you—almost any woman would!"

"I've been a coward. I haven't wanted to face my life, so I've faced my death instead. Just like you. We've both been running away from who we are by creating false identities of who we think we are. I've created my identity as a cancer patient, just like you've created your identity as a junkie. We've been hiding behind those identities, not transcending them. We're both cowards."

I sat down beside her on the piano bench and gave her a hug.

"I may be a coward, Daryl, but there's no way you are. You're the bravest woman I know."

"You don't know many women, then," she said, half laughing and half crying. "We *are* cowards, both of us. But cowardice is just a part of it. We ran away from ourselves because we had to. I wanted to survive and couldn't look at myself. So after all that chemo, I still clung to my identity as a cancer patient, because it's all I ended up with when they were through with me. At least when I'm running away, I'm doing my damnedest to keep going. Now the question I have to ask myself is, where am I going?"

And that's when it hit me. It had been years since I first ran away. And even though I'd never stopped running, I hadn't once asked myself where it was that I was going.

Even wild horses have a destiny. Why hadn't I found mine?

All that is real in our past is the love we gave and the love we received.
Everything else is an illusion.
—*Marianne Williamson*

Chapter 17

Spiral of Death

We practically lived at the hospital. I would grab a white lab coat and clipboard and accompany her to her treatments and tests, as if I belonged there. We giggled at the secret. No one ever questioned me. Maybe they knew how important it was for me to be there, but most likely, they were just too busy to notice. I liked thinking it was our secret.

We put up several posters in Daryl's hospital room, to give her something to focus on. One was of an old lady in a rocking chair holding up her middle finger. It was Daryl's statement, as if to say, "Fuck you, cancer." Fighting became our only hope for survival, each of us fighting to stay alive. I was fighting to get off drugs, and Daryl was fighting to stay on drugs. As long as she could do that, she was alive.

When we could, we went north to The Farm. We swam with the fishes and played catch with Daryl's prostheses. Music began to take the place of Street Horse. Our music was never ending. It made us laugh and it made us cry. Company came and went. Jay was around a lot more. He became our comic relief, laughing deep in his belly at the absurdity of our connection to life and death and each other and our refusal to give up. He even wrote a song about our not giving up, and we all cried together.

I slept downstairs to be closer to Daryl. I had to get up several times in the night to check on her and give her meds. Some days, she couldn't get out of bed at all. Those were the bad days, but they were healing nonetheless. We sat together, telling stories, singing softly, remembering the future just up ahead.

"Next time we come up, we need to make a recording," I said as we were packing to go back to Toronto. "We have enough songs for an album and—," but Daryl cut me off.

"I won't be coming back," she said, looking out the window to the garden we'd planted. "This is my last time at The Farm." A tear slowly trickled down her face, and I knew she was speaking the truth.

"Daryl, don't say that; you don't know how you'll be feeling," but in answer, she stepped closer to me and gave me a hug.

"It's okay," she said. "Let's go." I looked at her, not sure if I should protest or accept what she'd just said. Daryl wasn't coming back to The Farm. Ever.

"You're really good at this," Daryl said as I read over her lab report and explained to her what was happening with her cancer cells. "You should go back to school."

"Don't be crazy," I said. "I have enough to do just taking care of you." But I couldn't deny that there was a part of me that had already been thinking the same thing. I wanted to learn everything I possibly could about the devastating cancer demon that was eating away my best friend, cell by cell.

"It's not crazy," Daryl said. "After all, you found time to go the bars when you were addicted. Now that you've stopped doing heroin, you have more time than ever to go back to school. Promise me you'll do that."

I promised and enrolled in a lab technology course at the local community college. If I could do just one thing to better understand what was happening to Daryl, then I was going to do it.

I had to laugh. My parents had always planned for me to go to the best schools, yet here I was, amazed at myself for finally enrolling in a community college! It wasn't the Ivy Leagues, but as far as I was concerned, it was something even better. I'd been schooled in the streets for years, and now I was returning to a world of books and ideas that might not be as exciting as some of the crazy nights and days I'd been caught up in, but the mysteries contained in those books and ideas might somehow save Daryl's life, or at the very least, somehow make sense of her death—if it ever came to that.

It couldn't come to that. There was just no way.

It was Mother's Day. Years had gone by without contact with my parents. So much had changed since then. I wanted them to know I was back in school. I wanted them to know I'd gotten off drugs. I wanted them to know I loved them.

I knew I had to be the one to reach out, to let them know I was okay. If I did that, they might love me.

I felt beads of sweat on my forehead and upper lip as I dial the number I'd memorized for life.

I can do it. I can do it. I can do it.

After three rings, just as I was about to hang up, she answered.

"Hello? Hello? Who is this?" she asked in her familiar screech.

I could barely speak. Just those few words sent me careening back in time.

"It's me," I said in a voice so soft and frightened that it might have come from a small child. "It's Claire. I wanted to wish you Happy Mother's Day."

There was a painfully silent delay.

"I said, it's Claire," I said again, waiting for an acknowledgement.

"What are you calling here for?" she said as if I were selling something. "I told everybody you were dead. Don't call here again." Then all I heard was the dial tone.

I sat quietly holding the phone in my hand, wondering what had just happened. In less than twenty words the wounds of the past had reopened as painfully as if my soul had been slit open with a knife. Every child wants their mother to love them, even the ones who have hurt you or don't want you. But she had killed me in her heart, as surely as if I'd never been born.

Something was missing in her heart space. And because of that, something was missing in my heart space. I had hoped to fill that space, even temporarily, by some recognition that I mattered. But it would never come.

I'd tell no one I called her, just as she would tell no one I called, not even my father. It would be another secret.

Several days passed. Then one evening I returned late from school to find Daryl sitting at her desk, pen in hand. Something felt terribly wrong. The room was heavy with pain. Usually, I found her at the piano.

"What's wrong?" I asked, afraid to hear the answer. "What are you writing?" I sat down across from Daryl, and my soft, concerned eyes looked into the mirrors of her soul so heavy with pain.

"This is my will," she said. "I know that this time I won't make it. I want you to have The Farm."

I exhaled sharply.

"Oh my God, Daryl, no." I could feel the blood draining from my face, and I felt a chill pass through me. "Are you sure? Really sure? About not making it, I mean."

"I saw the doctor today. I'm sure," she said in a whisper.

We sat together crying and talking, trying to come to terms with the ending of this chapter—the ending we had no music for.

Over the next few weeks, dates on the calendar changed as fast as the number of cancer cells increased. Daryl was dying. Along with her life, the cancer cells were gobbling up our relationship. Angry words spilled out of pill bottles stacked one on top of the other at her bedside. Peace and tranquility turned into hostility and chaos. We yelled at each other. We said mean, hurtful things. At the very time we should have let go of all our anger, all our conflicts, we fertilized them with our fears. We were so afraid of the death that was coming between us, the death that was taking Daryl away, that we turned on each other as if somehow the other had made it all happen.

I couldn't sleep. I couldn't eat. We both got sicker. And Daryl got stranger.

She began yelling, over nothing at all, or worrying obsessively over things she normally wouldn't have even noticed. She was increasingly confused. It was more than just being under stress. I was worried something was really wrong.

Finally, I made an appointment with Daryl's psychiatrist. She'd been seeing him to cope with the pain and fear of cancer and the emptiness left inside her when her own mother, like mine, had turned away.

He ushered me into his office with a hug and pointed to a large leather chair, just like the one in the old library. I sat, hoping to find the comfort I once did in my father's chair. But I didn't. This chair was cold and unmoving.

We were silent, my eyes watching him, waiting. His eyes avoided mine by looking around the room as he tapped his pen on the blank writing tablet. I wanted to grab it out of his hand and make him stop. *This is crazy. Maybe I should start. Okay, I'll start.*

"Well, I wanted to tell you about some changes in Daryl's behavior," I said. "She's easily angered and getting mean, not like she used to be at all. It's become really difficult to care for her at home." I thought if he understood how her moods were changing, how much she was yelling, he might be able to adjust her meds or something. He just nodded as I spoke.

After a short silence, he said, "That's to be expected." He continued patiently. "Her behavior is erratic and unpredictable because the cancer is in her bones and brain now. The cancer interacts with the drugs to cause her to hallucinate and become delusional. You're with her the most, so it's not surprising that you're the frequent target."

I nodded and babbled some more about how she was acting. Then, wearing a pretend smile, he scribbled something on his prescription pad and handed it to me. My time was apparently up.

"Here, take these; they'll help with the stress," he said, ushering me to the door and closing it silently on his perfect world.

I looked down at the slip of paper. The prescription wasn't for Daryl. He'd written it for me.

I filled the prescription at a pharmacy near his office and sat on a bench in the Village. I watched as people rushed past with what suddenly felt like a sense of urgency, as if they had somewhere terribly important to be and it wasn't wherever they were. No one smiled. No one looked at the girl on the bench crying with a pill bottle in her hand.

I poured a few of the little yellow pills onto my palm. Everybody was taking them. They used to call them tranquilizers, but now they were calling them "anti-anxiety meds." My finger rolled them around like I used to do on the buttons of Dad's chair.

I'll be okay. I'll be okay. I'll be okay.

Hand to mouth they disappeared like Chiclets. I thought of a Donavon song about being mellow yellow. A smile pushed through my tears. I merged with the plastic people, rushing to nowhere. As I hummed the song to myself, I swallowed more little yellow pills and smiled at the strangers. They looked away.

Several days later I woke up, clothed in hospital garb and locked in a room. They told me I was found unconscious at the railway station, covered in blood. I remembered nothing. I nearly died on the outside, and now that I'd been found, I felt as if I were dead on the inside.

A young doctor pushed into my room, his demeanor all cheerful and smiley.

"So, how's my little patient today?" he asked in a patronizing tone. "Do you remember what happened?"

"No. Should I?" I snapped. But before he could answer, I told him, "I'm okay now. Get me my clothes. Please." My wrists were bandaged and it hurt to move them. I wasn't sure why.

"You know," he said, "you did a really good job there. I understand you're a musician. I'm sorry, but I don't believe you'll ever play the piano again. You severed all the tendons."

The corners of his mouth turned up ever so slightly, as if he found pleasure in what he'd just announced. My identity, I realized, was no longer junkie. I had officially become a mental patient.

"I don't think so," I replied. "Nothing will keep me from playing, ever. You don't know me."

"We'll see," he said confidently and flipped to the next page of his clipboard. "Oh, by the way, your parents are here, so get yourself presentable."

"Are you kidding me?" I asked. "I don't want to see them. Why would you call them?" My heart was racing in anger. I was horrified they'd contacted them. It had been years since I'd seen them. And after that Mother's Day call, I didn't expect to ever have contact with my mother again.

"Where's Daryl? I want to see *her*, not them," I said.

"Sorry," he replied. "I'm afraid both me and Daryl's doctor don't want you to have any contact with her right now."

My mood slipped into darkness. I didn't understand.

He stood to leave, declaring, "I'll get your parents now. Try to be nice. They drove a long way." With that he slipped out and into his hospital world.

I didn't bother washing my face. If there had been a window, I would have tried to escape. But I was trapped in there, with no way out. I couldn't even lock it.

The door swung open and instantly the energy changed. I said nothing, but inside I wanted to scream.

My father stood in the doorway, looking to the side of me, afraid to make eye contact. My mother had no such fears; she took three steps and was instantly at my bedside. She was dressed in her best clothes, as I knew she would be. She wore a plaid suit made from the finest wool with a sweater to match the exact color purple of the piping around the buttons. She clutched her black leather purse smartly over her arm, just like in the catalogues. And I noticed she was wearing new glasses. They had pointed corners with fake jewels. But nothing could detract from the thick lenses that made her eyes so huge they filled the rims, looking almost as if they were wobbling in her eye sockets like an evil bobble-head doll.

"I'm so embarrassed," she hissed, brushing imaginary lint off of her jacket. "I can't believe you would do this to us. Don't think you are coming back with us, young lady, because you're not. I told you before, you're dead to us." She turned abruptly toward the door.

"Let's go. I don't know why we had to be here anyway." Without another look, my father followed her out, closing the door to the world behind them.

I shrank into the blue, flowered bedspread, pretending it was a garden surrounded by blue concrete walls.

I traced the outline of the blue flowers with my pointer finger— around and around and around.

I want to go home. I want to go home. I want to go home.
I'll be okay. I'll be okay. I'll be okay.

The garden soaked up my tears as I thought about what to do next. Where do I belong now if even my own parents won't take me?

A few weeks later they let me check out of the hospital, and I went straight home to see Daryl. When I reached our apartment on Hazelton, the first thing I saw was a huge "For Rent" sign in the front window.

That's odd. I wonder who has moved.

The moment I stepped into the front hall, I immediately knew something had changed. Gone were the warm smells of dinner cooking. Gone were the different fragrances from around the world as incense burned. Gone were sounds of guitars being plucked and pianos played. With dread filling my heart, I climbed the stairs and opened the door to our apartment. Everything was gone.

I stood there, staring in disbelief. Daryl was gone. She had just up and moved while I was in the hospital. There was no furniture, no piano, and no plants. There was no life at all in the apartment. My life on Hazelton has been wiped out as if it never even existed. Who would do such a thing? Was Daryl that far gone that she could just move out like that without any thought at all of me? My heart filled with pain as I absorbed another loss.

I had nowhere to go except back in time, back to my other world downtown. I didn't really belong in Daryl's world, after all. Her sudden departure was proof of that. Once more I had to begin my life over with nothing, nothing except a heart full of pain. How could she do that to me?

A couple of weeks later I was sitting on a bench in the Village, still numb from shock, wondering what happened to make Daryl just up and abandon me like that. What had they told her?

"Hey. Where the hell have you been?"

The gruff voice snapped me back to reality. I looked up and saw Jay standing with his hands on his hips, spit on his beard sparkling like little diamonds.

"Why weren't you there? Where were you?" he demanded, his bushy eyebrows forming the letter V.

"Why wasn't I where? What are you talking about, Jay? Do you know where my things are? Where's Daryl?" The questions came rushing out. I paused only when I noticed Jay's eyes were wet and misty.

"Jay, what's going on? Tell me!" A dagger of silence pierced my words, and in an instant, I knew the answer.

"Daryl died." The words hit me like a punch in my gut. "And where were you? Why weren't you at the funeral?" Jay sat down beside me, his questions nothing but rhetorical barbs he felt he had to sling before falling apart himself.

"What do you mean she died? Jay, *no!* Tell me she's not gone!" I demanded, as if I could force him to take it all back. But I knew it was too late. There was nothing either of us could do.

I began to sob, and my words tumbled out from my choking throat in gasps.

"I didn't know! Why didn't you find me? Oh my God, Jay!" I dropped my head into my hands and wept.

"We looked everywhere for you," he said. "She was asking about you all the time. We didn't know where you went." He pulled me close, and we held each other tightly.

We sat like that on the bench, both of us crying; a sad young girl being held by a big-bellied, big-bearded musician. People crossed the street to avoid walking by.

Jay told me Daryl had fallen down the stairs and broken a hip while I was in the hospital, and when they took her to the operating room, she died. Five months before her twenty-ninth birthday, so close to the five-year mark of life with cancer. He had my guitar, but both of our moms cleaned out the apartment and everything else was gone. Everything. I had nothing anymore, just my guitar. And I had nothing of Daryl, not even a scrap of paper.

I couldn't believe it had ended, just like that. She was not there. I was not there. We were both alone. I felt shattered like broken glass. The tears became endless.

The Continental girls tried to be supportive, but they really couldn't understand. My chance at a different life had just died.

When I asked about my music and the will, I was told to talk to Daryl's rich uncle, who was a lawyer. When I went to see him, he just laughed and told me to get lost. He said she'd left no will. I knew that wasn't true, because I'd seen it. I had watched her sign it.

But I didn't really care about The Farm. Without Daryl, it was just a piece of property. I really just wanted our music, my music. It would mean nothing to anyone else. I pleaded my case in his cold leather office in between my tears, but it was to deaf ears. He has destroyed the will. My life on Hazelton Avenue had simply disappeared.

*Out beyond ideas of wrong doing and right doing there is a field.
I'll meet you there. When the soul lies down in that
grass, the world is too full to talk about.*
—*Rumi*

Chapter 18

Broken

I found a new place to crash around the corner from Norm's Café and the street where Daryl and I first lived. Fifteen floors of lonely people stacked one on top of another, room by room, and I felt like the loneliest of them all. I tried to get a job, but no one would hire me when they realized the only place I'd ever worked was in a prison.

One day a fat, greasy shop owner followed me home and waited for me to come outside. There was a time I would have taken such attention as genuine, but I was no longer naïve. By this time, I knew exactly what he wanted from me. And I knew that he had nothing that I wanted.

I spent the nights back at the Continental where I soon acquired new battle wounds. Each one told a story. A split in my nose told one story. The dangling black threads that tickled my lip told another. Nights got pretty wild at the Continental, and with no one to go home to, I didn't much care. I stayed away from the Street Horse, but after drinking all day, emotions ran free. I didn't talk a lot about my feelings after Daryl died. It was safer that way.

I read the classified ads daily, but it seemed like I wasn't qualified for anything. I was especially drawn to the ones that advertised for nurses and wished I could apply, but that would take a nursing degree, which I obviously didn't have. Then one morning I became excited when I saw an advertisement for a job as a designer in a sportswear factory. I had always been pretty artistic, so I called and they invited me in for an interview. I scrubbed myself clean of the Continental night, dressed myself in suitable attire, and headed out to Spadina Avenue to the fashion district.

Sammy, the boss, showed me around the cutting room, which was busy with a dozen weather-beaten Italian women snipping and sewing away. He guided me around the sewing tables with his hand on my waist. The Italian ladies looked up briefly and shook their heads as we passed. I felt their judgment as clearly as I felt Sammy's hand on my waist.

Sammy was also Italian, and he smelled of cigars and pepperoni. His hair was greasy and he kept pushing it back with his free hand. When he talked, his mouth glistened with gold. Root canals, I thought, though I knew in Sammy's mind they were status symbols.

"This is my office. Come on in and shut the door," he said, waving me inside.

There was a large easel with drawings and a rack of clothes hanging beside it. He pulled out a navy blue suit and proudly shoved it in my hands. "Here. Put it on. I want to see what you look like in it," he instructed, smiling from ear to ear.

"You want me to wear it? You mean like a model?" I asked.

"Yes. Just like a model. You're pretty enough to be one," he replied, pulling the dusty beige screen aside. He licked his lips and pushed me behind the screen.

"You would have to do this a lot, you know, and you might have to go out with the buyers dressed in my outfits." His words slithered over the top of the screen and covered me with disgust.

Before I could answer, he slipped behind the screen. The smell of his aftershave mixed with wine nauseated me, and I broke into a sweat.

His hands with their dirty fingernails gripped my shoulders and he whispered, "Shh. Don't make a sound. Nobody will know." Without taking his eyes off of my breasts, he slipped his hands between my legs and grinned.

"Get the hell away from me!" I yelled as I pushed his hand away. He fell into the screen, cursing. I pulled on my jeans. Still wearing the navy blue jacket from the rack, I ran out the door as fast as I could, pushing shoppers out of my way. My feet hardly touched the concrete as I flew up Spadina Ave and turned right onto Dundas Street. I was heading straight for the Continental. My breath came in deep heaves as I pushed the heavy wooden door to the bar open and raced into the comforting arms of my Continental family and my Street Horse friends.

Something inside me had broken. Not only was my heart shattered, but my spirit was fractured as well. I couldn't trust anyone. They all wanted the same thing from me. My soul was all I had left. I had to protect that or I would slip away into nothing. I sat in the dark bar in my private corner, drawing horse heads out of beer glass circles. Where was Heart Horse?

Disappointment crept across me like little bugs crawling under my skin. No matter how much I drank, the sensation would not go away. I dug my nails into my flesh, but I still couldn't stop the crawling disappointment. It had become a part of me.

A few days later, back at the tower of lonely people that was my new home, I met a new friend. His name was Ben. He was the only other young person living in the tower; everyone else had already decayed with age—their hair had gone gray and their teeth were gone before they even hit fifty.

Ben and I rode the elevator together a few times and politely nodded and smiled. When our eyes met, we both noticed that they held the same stories of sadness. We shared a look of haunting pain.

Day after day I walked the city looking for work. I finally found a job at a dry cleaner. When I explained where I got my experience, the owner didn't back away. He said he was happy to help. I waited for him to make a move on me, but he didn't. I finally had a job, a real job.

My days became like everyone else's. Like "the plastic people" I used to mock, I was going to work every day, eating and sleeping on schedule. I stayed away from the familiar downtown haunts and the faces that I knew. The Continental and Norm's beckoned me as I walked past them to get to work, but I never entered. I knew if I opened that door even once, I'd return to life downtown.

But I also knew I didn't really belong in the new world of my workday. I couldn't relate to people that had lived in comfort and not experienced the kind of pain I'd been through. Somehow that pain didn't just make me feel different. It had actually *made* me different, set me apart from the world in a weird and inexplicable way. I knew if I spoke about my life, I would be judged and rejected, and knowing that, I remained silent. I was accepted as long as who I really was and what I'd really done in my short life wasn't spoken aloud.

By working and living with such a routine, something else happened. I no longer wanted to be part of my old downtown life. I didn't seem to fit in there anymore; I didn't feel as if I fit in anywhere, for that matter. My heart space had become a puzzle with missing pieces, and all of the pieces I was finding as I tried to put my life together somehow didn't fit. I didn't fit. I rode the buses with the plastic people watching me, their frozen eyes. But I couldn't see anything other than empty spaces and nothing felt familiar.

I missed Daryl.

Ben and I started getting to know each other. He was studying to be an ambulance driver. Since I had once had plans of working in a hospital, and I'd certainly had lots of rides in ambulances, we had that in common.

But something inside me had fundamentally changed. I noticed things he said or did that left me a bit concerned. In the past, I never would have noticed these things, and if I did, I wouldn't have viewed them with concern; I would have enjoyed them. But now I noticed that he drank too much and drove too fast, and I wondered about all of the pills he kept lined up on his desk. I looked at Ben, no different from me in so many ways, and instead of enjoying our common bond of drugs and drinking, I recoiled.

I had entered the real world, where that old life didn't belong. In the past the thought of living a life of routine was worse than death. But now routine was critical to my survival, so I followed it, never straying too far out of the boundaries I'd marked for myself.

On my way home from work one evening, I stopped at a different bar called Charlie's. The Continental was just down the street. My feet wanted to go there, but my heart held back. It was all I could do to resist. That chapter needed to be closed.

I found a corner where I sat with a warm beer and wished I were somewhere else. Over the bar a silent television played. My thoughts were louder than the television, but they formed no words. I watched anyway. It was a travel show about the wonders of a cross-Canada trip. Suddenly, there they were: the Rocky Mountains with Lake Louise dressed in green emeralds and the glistening snow-covered peaks of Banff. It was exactly where Uncle Willy told me I would go one day, the very place he said I'd find my own wild horse.

I knew it was time.

I made one last trip to The Farm, hitchhiking to northern Ontario in hopes that somehow I might find a whisper of Daryl's spirit still alive in our private sanctuary. I knew I was trespassing, that it wasn't mine, yet it felt like it was mine and I had to go back.

My hopes were shattered the moment I reached the road. The grass had grown back to the wild state we'd first found it. Windows were broken, and the doors were unlocked. Inside the house had been decimated. The furniture was either gone or demolished. The piano, gone. Our piles of music, gone. Our photo albums, gone. Porcupines had chewed up the hand-carved table, and someone had torn up everything they could get their hands on and strewn it across the room. Even the propane lights had been ripped off the wall.

I was just heartbroken. I dropped my backpack right there in the middle of the room where I stood, lowered myself to the floor, and sat there and cried. I don't know why I thought things would be intact, just as it was when we left it, with the dishes on the table and the bed in the living room.

Daryl was really gone, and that part of my life would never come back. I had lost it.

I slept in the house one last night, and then I hiked to the road and stuck out my thumb. Westward.

There are many paths to wisdom,
But each begins with a broken heart.
—Leonard Cohen

Chapter 19

Mountains of Memories

I travelled for several days before reaching the foothills of the Canadian Rockies. As I climbed out of the cabin of the flatbed truck that brought me through that last, final stretch, I thanked the driver and began the long hike into the wild grasses and woods where I would, hopefully, find my horse. I was determined to find it, to look my own wild horse in the eye and claim it as my own.

Looking up, I become enveloped in the arms of an incomprehensible serenity that flowed from the mountains. Finally, I was free of the city. Finally, I was at peace.

I felt safe at last. I felt as if I were exactly where I should be, where I should have been all along, where I would wait for the wild horses to appear. I would know mine the moment that I saw it. I had no idea what I would do with such knowledge—it wasn't like I could just jump on its back and ride off into the sunset, as appealing as the idea was. But something powerful had brought me to this exact spot, something that transcended all the years of pain, abuse, and self-defeat. Something said to me, "Come to this spot, so that you might know yourself."

I'd travelled to this spot in my mind over and over again for so many years, visualizing this very valley—the circle of majestic mountains, the diamond-studded lake, the different shades of green and yellow grasses, and the tiny purple flowers that grew in patches. It was exactly as my Uncle Willy had described it.

I had memorized that moment before I even got here. I knew exactly where the highest mountain sat. I knew from which valley the horses would come thundering out. I knew the shadows of the setting sun and the designs that changed on the mountainsides as the night fell. I knew because all along Heart Horse had been pushing me there, nudging me out of the black, blood darkness of my past to direct me to this magical spot, as if he were showing me how to get home. All I had to do was pay attention.

"This journey is my gift to you, Heart Horse," I announced. How long had it been since I'd spoken aloud to Heart Horse? Would he even hear me after all this time?

We would find a horse of extraordinary grace, beauty, gentleness, spirit, and strength. I longed to feel and sense those qualities that I somehow knew were buried deep inside my own heart space, but I wasn't sure I could ever feel those qualities again, buried as they'd become over the last several years.

Wild horses might reveal them; they are poetry in motion. They recognize the true nature of others. Would they recognize such qualities inside me, or had Street Horse killed my own inner beauty?

I only knew that I would wait for as long as it took to hear them speak their wisdom.

I walked for four hours, my beat-up guitar and backpack bumping against my back with every step. I was exhausted physically, emotionally, and spiritually from the two and a half decades of my life. Every bone, cell, and fiber of my being longed for peace and just one safe and restful moment. I would have gone even further, but Heart Horse had awakened and was practically falling against my chest, urging me to stop. He was trying to tell me we had found the spot; we had made it.

My feet screamed in pain, and I had a raw, empty sensation in my belly from not eating, but I felt a lightness in my heart that had not been there before. I needed to sit and rest, and then hopefully my thoughts would clear and I would know the perfect spot where I would wait for the horses. My shoulders ached inside my bones and all through my muscles from carrying my entire world on my back.

In my backpack were the few things I called my own: another pair of blue jeans, the faded, tattered ones with a jagged slice across the knee like a scar; two T-shirts, both faded yellow like the sun's rays that surrounded me; and a red, plaid lumber jacket, so quintessentially Canadian. And I had my journals and sheets of music paper for writing my songs. I also brought along a paper bag filled with folded music paper on which I'd written the life lessons I had learned. Someday I hoped they would be sung.

Fortunately, I'd thought to bring along a sleeping bag. It wasn't new, but it was clean and it would keep me warm enough.

The most important thing I brought was my guitar. It was really the only thing I had that was worth any money. I tied it to my leg at night when I hitchhiked or slept outside, so that it wouldn't get stolen. Not because I was concerned about the cost of replacing it if it were stolen, but because I needed it. Music had become my lifeline and my best friend; losing my guitar would feel like losing the last scrap of connection I had to Daryl. This was the guitar we'd made our music on. This was the guitar that was always there for me when I felt alone and sad.

I had enough bread and peanut butter to last a few days, some apples the truck driver gave me, and a chocolate bar. I knew the mountain water was good to drink, so I'd be fine. It seemed like a lot. I would save the apples for the horses, I decided.

I dropped my right shoulder an inch or two, and the sweaty blue strap slipped down my arm. My guitar was strapped onto my pack, so I carefully shrugged off the left strap, caught the guitar, and gently lowered my world of possessions onto the lush and fertile table of this new world I'd discovered. Tilting back my head, I gazed up to the mountainsides and saw that their tops were frosted in crispy white snow. For the first time ever, I felt like an insurmountable weight has been lifted from my heart. I raised my hands toward the sky and sang at the top of my lungs.

"Hellooo... I'm here... hellooo... I'm here... hellooo... I'm here," I called out. My voice bounced back from the distant mountainside, reassuring me that I wasn't alone. I had myself. And Heart Horse.

As I faced the setting sun in the west, I could discern a line of trees at the base of the mountain range, directly in front of me. I couldn't tell how thick the line was, but I imagined it was maybe a mile through to the other side. To my left was a small lake, which was the reason I chose that spot to stay for the night. It was the end of summer, and it had been dry for a while, so I reasoned the horses would need to drink. There was a bit of green grass, the last of the season, poking through the drying grasses.

"If I were a wild horse," I said aloud to Heart Horse, "I would look for this valley too; don't you think? Look, the trees are a safe place for the horses to hide. They can run into one of the many smaller mountainous valleys and just disappear." The tree line was like the skyline of the city, all the buildings that provided a place for people to disappear into.

If I wanted to catch a wild horse, I knew I would have to think like one. That really wouldn't be difficult, I figured, since we shared a lot of similarities. Wild horses must fight a desperate battle to survive, just as I had learned to do. I knew if I could watch them, I'd see how miraculously they blended into their surroundings like chameleons. Like me.

Horses have a lot to teach about survival. Even a horse's physique is unique to survival. They have large hooves to carry them over marshes and to paw through the snow for feed. Most of them have short legs and are stocky with bodies made of pure muscle for strength and endurance. They use their noses to forage for food through the snow. It's all about survival.

I had known their struggle to survive since I, too, had learned to survive by adapting to my environment. And I realized that was what I must do in the wild if I wanted to capture the heart of a wild horse.

Finally, I dropped like a wilted flower to the ground and leaned my back against my pack. There was no noise—just the comforting sounds of nature after leaving the cacophony of the city. I closed my eyes and sucked in the sun-kissed mountain air. It was warm and yet at the same time had a clean, cool bite to it. It was not at all like the smog-filled gritty air that had been clogging my lungs for months. I opened one eye just a crack and looked out, just in case I was dreaming.

"Come on, Heart Horse. It's probably a good idea to fill the water bottle and try to find some wood to start a small fire before it gets dark," I said, again out loud. I thought if I kept speaking out loud to Heart Horse, he would stay this time. I had already lost enough; I didn't want to lose the only thing I had left that would protect me. If I kept on speaking to him, he might not vanish.

But I didn't move. The water could wait a minute or two. I lie back onto the ground and felt my body becoming one with it, sinking into it as if there was no separation between the earth and me. I let the sensation take over and recharge my body with the earth's energy—just for a while. Then I reached out and checked the few inches around my sweaty torso. What was once lush green grass had become sharp little straw spikes that jabbed my skin.

I knew by morning there would be a flat place. The spikes would be crushed into a perfect form-fitting bed. I'd slept in worse places, so I didn't mind. I had once slept in an alley underneath garbage bags. Another time I fell asleep on jagged rocks under a bridge. Once after sleeping all night in the park, I woke up soaking wet. So I could handle this place.

Letting my heavy eyelids close with a slight crack of vision just in case, I relaxed into the warm earth. A circling hawk let out a loud cry. She must have been the mountain's alarm system alerting the creatures that there was a stranger in their midst. I smiled in my heart. I knew that animals weren't like people. They would accept me, for I was a creature of the wild myself.

The air started to cool, and the sun began its dance further into the mountain peaks. There were still a few hours of daylight, enough to make my camp and settle in. In the morning, if I was lucky, the horses would come.

I reached into my pack, pulled out some bread, and began rolling it into tight little bread balls, just like when I was a kid. Then I opened a jar of peanut butter and scooped some up with a bread ball. I popped one in my mouth, chewed it up, and swallowed. Not bad, I decided as I popped another in my mouth. I ate several peanut-butter bread balls before stopping. I was still not full, but I had to make my provisions last as long as I could.

Heart Horse whinnied and jumped to attention. My arms immediately burst into goose bumps, and a shiver worked its way up my back.

Someone or something was watching me. I could feel it. My lungs pulled in a chest full of air. I strained to recognize horse smells. But I could only smell grass, no horses.

I needed to refocus, to concentrate on something other than my own imagination. It was time to write. I would write down everything I saw and experienced so that I could memorize each moment.

I carefully pulled out the weathered book filled with stories and secrets. The leather was soft with fine cracks like an old lady's wrinkles. I knew each and every wrinkle as if they were my own. I turned each page slowly until the last words I had written appeared. Pen to paper, the previous night's song flowed like a river onto the page.

After the first few lines, my mind wandered to the Horse Rules.

"Should I write them down now?" I asked Heart Horse. "Will it make them clear in my mind?" I inhaled the mountain air, as if it would give more meaning to my words, as if it would somehow make them crisper.

I loved the feeling of knowing I could just be myself around horses. That was something I'd learned from Heart Horse. With Heart Horse in my heart, I didn't feel judged or rejected; I felt loved and listened to. I'd created Heart Horse to fill that empty space inside me when I was just a little girl. As I got older, whenever I grew distant from him, the empty space grew greater, and I grew more distant from my true self. As I thought of him, Heart Horse gently swayed back and forth inside me, calming me just as he did when I was a child.

Shaking my head and readjusting myself on my seat, I forced my mind to refocus on the present and what I was doing. Was my wishful thinking creating faraway horse talk?

"Shh, Heart Horse, settle down," I whispered as I tilted my head to the left. My ears pulled in the vibrations coming from the forest. Nothing had changed—no movement, no sounds, no horses.

Okay. Focus. The rules. What are the rules? I knew that the leader was usually a mare.

"Isn't that interesting? A woman horse rules." I liked that about horses. They did what was best for their herd. The stallions were the protectors of their family. In a horse family, the mares were very kind and loving, even when they disciplined the other horses. As soon as they made them behave, they went back to being loving. That was why I said they didn't hold grudges.

I licked the dull tip of my pencil, a habit I had before writing anything down. The first rule appeared on the page, and I circled it. The first rule was always so easy.

"You need to be calm, because horses are really sensitive to the feelings of humans. Again, not like people I know."

> I'm curled up tight in a ball like a frightened turtle.
> "Get up you lazy brat! Go! Peel the potatoes. Now!" Tears slide down my already wet face. I uncurl to do as she says. I'm so sad. So broken, so alone. Someday I won't be. Not right now, but someday. That's a secret.

"Rule number two is that you move very slowly toward them so you don't scare them."

> The house had floors that talked. Each step I took told its own story. If I wanted to get into the library to my wall, I had to be so careful, so she didn't know what I was doing. Right foot there, slide. Left foot

there, slide. Right foot there, slide. She never knew how I did it without her knowing. She won't ever know. Not now, not ever. That's my secret.

"Rule number three is that you mustn't stare. They feel threatened if you do that." Heart Horse reared his body high in agreement, landing on a rib with a sharp jab. I understood that feeling too.

When mother was angry she had a way of putting her mouth in a straight line, really pinched and tight. Then she stared right into my eyes. That usually meant she was going to hit. I used to say my silent verses in my mind when she did that. I'm okay. I'm okay. I'm okay. You can't hurt me. Not anymore. Not forever. She never knew. That was my secret.

"Rule number four is that you have to talk very quietly and soothingly to them so that you show them you aren't a threat."

Sometimes when I'm behind Daddy's chair, I whisper when I do my counts when I circle the buttons. Softly so she won't hear. It makes it work better, and I have learned to be quiet. I won't have to always. I do now, but not forever. That's my secret.

"Rule number five is common sense. You don't make any sudden movements or you'll scare them away."

As her hand cuts through the air toward me, I feel myself shrinking and use my hands to cover my face. Startled, I run as fast as I can to the back of the garden and slide down the hill far away from her. I take it, for now, but not forever. That's my secret.

There are really specific rules about getting close.

"When you inch your way toward them, you slowly turn sideways. In horse language, that means, 'Come to me.' That's number six, you know. You let them smell you, and maybe, only maybe, you can reach out to touch their neck. If you do that, you keep your fingers together. Did you get that?" I was talking to Heart Horse, but he didn't respond.

The rules to taming wild horses all made sense to me. They were almost the same as the ones I'd learned to survive among the wild herds of the city's streets.

I could have continued about how to put a halter on, but since I didn't have one, I decided to stop. Deep inside my heart there was an ache that made it hard to think about the horses. I knew I couldn't stay there forever. And knowing that, I felt somehow lost and alone, even as I felt such joyous peace and excitement to have finally reached the Rockies, where I knew the wild horses roamed.

Warm salty trickles of pain wandered down my cheeks. I'd come so far, yet my heart felt so hollow. It ached to be filled up. I'd been searching constantly for anything that might fill the holes up, for as long as I could remember. And it was that search, I realized, that had led me to Street Horse.

The warm sun soothed me and began to erase my cloudy thoughts. I quickly wiped the saltwater from my face with my shirt. I seldom cried, especially since Daryl died. I was afraid if I let myself cry again, I might never stop; it was like opening a door that would never shut again.

With a snap of the cover, I closed my journal, shutting those thoughts inside with my writing. Beads of sweat gathered on my forehead. My shirt stuck to my back, soaking up the droplets running down my neck. I wiggled my boot off by pushing my toes against the heel. My feet were too swollen to get the boots off without a struggle. I reached down and pulled my left boot-encased foot across my knee and started to wiggle and pull, wiggle and pull, wiggle and pull.

Finally, with a sudden release, my foot was free. I switched sides and pulled off the other boot. I inspected the damage from the heat and hours of walking and began to peel off my sock. Like a slow striptease, the sock released its captive toes.

No wonder I couldn't get the boot off. My toes were swollen and blistered. There was an area along my big toe that looked like raw meat. But it would do no good to focus on it; in a couple of days it would be healed. I glanced sideways over to the lake, anticipating how great the icy water would feel when I slipped into it. My feet would thank me then.

With both feet now free and naked, my eyes stole a look at what would be my home for the night. I sat alone in a world of space—alone with my guitar, surrounded by the mountains and the lake, the trees and the grasses, knowing that somewhere out there were horses: the Wind Horses, the Heart Horses, the Spirit Horses.

I felt a shiver of delight work its way up my tired body, recharging places that had been depleted of energy. I could almost taste the dust and feel the ground rumble as the horses charged out of the valley. But that was only my imagination; until it became real, all I had was my imagination.

I closed my eyes and imagined the snorts, wild eyes, and flowing manes of the horses my Uncle Willy had promised would one day be my own. Of course, I was grown now and knew that I could not take home a wild horse. But something had led me there, to that open space in the mountains where wild horses roamed, and I was determined to find my horse to learn the secrets it held for me, whatever those secrets might be.

Suddenly, I had a wonderful idea, and in an instant I was up on my feet. I tore off my clothes, pulled the elastic off of my waist-long braid, and shook my head, freeing my own mane. As if one with my imaginary Wind Horses, I galloped and laughed and felt as free and beautiful as the wildest, most breathtaking horse of all.

For a brief moment I realized what a sight I must have been, racing around naked in the mountain air shaking my long hair out as it flowed behind me. But I didn't care. There was no one else around. I was safe. I was free.

I galloped to the shores of the crystal lake, and without a thought I charged in. That's what a Wind Horse would do, so that is what I did. It was icy cold, and I could feel Heart Horse start to gallop inside my chest.

The first few feet of shoreline were mossy with sharp pebbles and shockingly frosty cold. I stumbled trying to keep my balance. I waded ten feet out, my legs freezing cold, when in an instant, I sunk into the clear depths of the bottomless lake.

I watched as the lake bottom moved under my feet, pulling me into its world of mud and weeds. I let my naked body sink. Slowly I came up for air, watching in awe as the surface sparkled with millions of glittering diamonds. What a delicious sensation it was to let myself become a part of the elements that surrounded me. As I pushed the icy water away and glided effortlessly to the middle, I knew I was meant to be there, to experience the sensation of being utterly, wildly, free, if only for that perfect, solitary moment.

A slimy rope of weeds grabbed at my ankle, but I kicked it away. With each breaststroke pushing me further from shore, I pushed away my fears of the unknown. I swam in the silky cool water like an undersea mermaid, making my way to the other side without ever disturbing the surface. As I watched the tree line come closer, I sensed there were eyes following my water ballet. I didn't get the sense they were human, so I felt no fear.

But I was curious.

Could it be? Could it possibly be one of the wild horses that I have searched for, yearned for for so long? Or had my imagination finally become so real that I couldn't even tell what was actually happening to me and what I was only imagining? I realized I didn't know the answer. But I had finally reached the shore.

Imagination is the first step toward action.
You have to be able to hope before you move forward.
Otherwise you are always acting out of fear.
—Gloria Steinem

Chapter 20

Nature's Freedom

As I climbed out of the water and onto some rocks, my wet foot slipped and without warning, I crashed to the base of a rock. My arms flailed outward to soften the landing, but my efforts were futile as my chin hit the edge of a large sitting rock.

"Ouch! Damn!" My words pierced the silent air. A sharp jolt of pain shot up my face as a spurt of ruby red blood juice spilled over the rock. "Oh well," I said aloud, "it's just one more battle wound." I'd absorbed enough of those in my short lifetime to know that the pain would pass.

I slowly pushed myself back to a standing position.

"Nothing broken, thank God," I said. I had told no one where I was going, and I wasn't likely to encounter anyone for a very long time. If I broke a bone or was seriously injured, it could be disastrous.

I should have told someone where I would be, or at least brought along a first-aid kit, I thought, realizing the foolishness of my secret quest into the wild.

Gingerly, I sat back down on the largest rock and watched with fascination as the ruby blood juice made little patterns on my bare skin.

> I'm eight. Around and around she chases me. The hand mirror is swinging wildly back and forth trying to reach my skin.
>
> "I'll get you, and when I do!" The hand mirror hits my eyebrow, slicing it open and spilling bright red blood that immediately drops onto my pristine dress front. "Now look what you've done!" she screams in that pitchy voice. "You made your dress dirty! Go! Wash it right now!"
>
> At least it's over I think to myself, and it didn't hurt. That's not what she wanted. That's my secret.

Warm blood juice oozed between my fingers as I tried to hold the wound together. I was reminded that things might look unthreatening and safe, but they could bring unexpected pain. I lifted my palm from the wound and felt with my fingers. The blood had stopped dripping.

Carefully and with extra caution, I picked my way over the smaller rocks, as I readied for the swim back to where I'd set up camp.

Once I reached the water's edge, I tiptoed in, savoring the ice waves as they lapped around my fiery hot ankles. Waves of shivers climbed up my legs. My chin was pulsating with a stinging sensation that matched Heart Horse's galloping anticipation. Once the water was deep enough, my body slid into the icy bath. This time the water surrounded me like a python, squeezing out my breath in a loud whoosh.

"Okay! You won't get me!" I yelled at the imaginary snake compressing me in its coil. "One, two, three, under we go!" The bottom became my diving board, and with a "Yippee!" I dove in.

My foot hit a big rock, hard, but I ignored the pain. Using it as a springboard I pushed upward and burst out of the water with great finesse and a loud splash.

"Hey! Anybody see that?" I yelled to the tree line. "Just like the synchronized swimmers, good, eh?" Arms slicing the water like a hot knife through butter, my pain dissolved with each stroke. In one glide, arms together, my water body rolled over, and I settled on my back. Relaxing into the water's arms, my eyelids slowly shut out the sun. The water held me gently, safely like the old brown chair in my father's study.

> As I sink into the brown leather cushion, a loud whoosh sound squeezes out around me. When the air rushes out, I breathe in my dad's smells: a bit of musty air mixed with pipe smells and Old Spice shaving cream. I feel safe here. The chair wraps me in a warm leather hug. I like hugs. That's my secret.

I flipped back onto my stomach and swirled around the edges of the lake, looking for any signs of horses, but I didn't see any animals at all, except for a few birds passing through the sky. Far away I could see a hawk circling something in the distance, and I wondered what it could be.

I climbed out of the lake and assessed my situation. My chin was no longer bleeding, but I could feel a big crack along my chin line. I wondered if it would leave a scar. I was covered in so many scars.

Back at camp, I climbed back into my jeans and pulled out my remaining clean shirt. As I shoved my toes deep inside my boots, a chill ran up my spine. Again I had that sense that someone or something was watching me.

"Geez, Claire," I said to myself, "are you getting paranoid or what?"

I squeezed the water out of my redone braid and hiked toward the trees. At the forest's edge there was an opening like a gate made of tree branches. I poked my head in and was struck by the deafening silence inside the cool, dark world. Soft sun lines were spaced at random intervals where the light crawled through the spaces, illuminating bits and pieces of the forest landscape like twinkling lights of gold.

I quietly stepped into the magical forest world. Taking a big breath, I smelled the different vegetation that surrounded me. The pine trees had a different smell from the mossy logs. The wet leaves smelled different from the pine needles. It was almost as if each shade of green had its own smell.

I remembered my dad's pipe smells, the chair smells, the library smells, and especially my Mother's smell. Survival teaches us to pay attention to smells. I have learned to smell fear and hate as acutely as a wild animal.

The pine needle floor cushioned every step, and as each foot settled, it made no sound. As I reached out my arms, I gently touched the trees on either side. Some were soft with mossy clothes, and some were sticky with sap and had rough jackets. Whatever their texture, each was perfect.

I stepped slowly, reveling in the quiet and peacefulness. Stepping over twigs and branches, I made my way through the dense undergrowth. Ahead there was a large pine tree base surrounded by a bush of wild Alberta roses. Amidst the many greens the vivid pink and white flowers jumped out as a surprise, a burst of vibrant beauty in such a dark, cool place.

Dozens of tiny pink buds covered the stubby bush. Only a few had opened with a burst of deep pink color, reminding me of the old perfume bottles in the library bookcases.

> The cases hold beautiful books filled with words I want to read and covers I long to touch. I want to trace the printing and explore the mysteries inside, but I can't. There are perfume bottles that are a warm rose color, and I always wonder if there is still perfume in them and what it might smell like. I long to touch them, too. I can't, not now. I will someday. I know it. That's my secret.

From a place as deep as those memories came a heavy sigh. I sat down on the jagged top seat of the tree and reached out to pull the rose shrub closer so I could inhale its fragrant smells. My fingers caressed the delicate petals.

"How have you survived?" I asked the pink flower. I fingered the soft petals, and Heart Horse puffed up and snorted, letting me know that I was like the wild rose. Despite the darkness in my life, I would bloom. My mouth crinkled up at the corners in a smile. The tiny petals were moist with forest dew, its skin so soft and fragile yet so strong in other ways. "Pure perfection," I whispered, bending down to kiss a small but perfect bud.

Suddenly, a loud crunching of branches startled me back to reality. Fast crunches, as if something was trying to break out of the underbrush. My eyes swiveled back and forth, up and down. They saw nothing. Heart Horse galloped wildly, trying to escape his fear of the unknown.

The crunches faded into the distance, and Heart Horse regained his composure and slowed his pace accordingly.

"It's probably just a tiny forest animal," I reassured him. Everything sounded loud when it erupted from total silence; I could hear even my own heart beating against my rib cage.

Cool forest air sucked up the excess heat. A slick layer of sweat covered my body.

"Nothing. Nothing but trees," I said, under my breath.

Each footstep took me deeper into the green wonderland. Time was immeasurable. I had no idea how long I'd been there, but I knew I had to get back soon, before it grew dark.

I had walked too far, I realized, and if I didn't hurry, I would find myself in a pitch-black forest. I had to get back to camp.

Faster, faster, go faster.

With each breath, urgency filled my lungs.

"Sun air. I need sun air," I whispered to Heart Horse. Suddenly, as if he'd heard me and parted the forest curtain just for me, a burst of light hit me and the cool darkness turned to brilliant warmth on my face.

A sunbeam bounced over my shoulder into the forest behind, just as I hit the open field. Without any prompting, my feet began a dance. Giggling like the schoolgirl I once was, so very long ago, Heart horse and I galloped and danced in the sunbeams.

The heat of the setting sun left beads of sweat that dripped down my forehead, leaving little pathways over my cheeks. A soft, warm breeze tickled my face, just as the quiet was punctuated with a faraway bird song. I broke into a run through the open grasses, back to my campsite. Everything was right where I had left it.

My guitar lay beside my bag, as if waiting my return. My eager arms reached for her and brought her to my lap. I held her neck gently with love. Like a faithful old friend that always loved me, she responded with a note or two from her tightly wound metal strings. My long fingers danced over the strings, just as they used to do on the ivory piano keys. My body swayed as I shut my eyes and played to the mountains, trees, and horses I knew were watching.

The once warming sun had begun its descent over the mountain tips. The air was turning to an evening chill, bringing goose bumps to the surface of my arms. I set the guitar down and started a fire to warm me through the night, building it just as I was taught in Girl Guides. Always be prepared.

Night songs began to echo from the hills. In the far distance the haunting howls of wolves talking back and forth to each other played on. In minutes the sun completely disappeared, and darkness laid its night blanket over me.

I crawled into my frosty sleeping sack and squished my jacket into a pillow under the crook of my neck. Focusing on a single star twinkling brighter than all the others, my lids struggled to stay open. But in an instant they fluttered closed, shutting out the stars. The last melody I remembered was the wolves' night song and a fire crackling in the background.

"Come to the edge," he said.
They said, "We are afraid."
"Come to the edge," he said.
They came.
He pushed them… and they flew.
—Guillaume Apollinaire

Chapter 21

Magic Is Real

Somewhere faraway in my mind, I could hear soft snorts and grunts like a background melody. My eyes snapped open in alarm, and Heart Horse jumped from a walk to a racing gallop.

The morning fog was thick and heavy. I searched the space around me, square by square. Was it real? Or was it my imagination? I thought I could hear them, the horses, but was I only dreaming? Where were they? It was still too dark to see.

Heart Horse was galloping in circles, kicking at my chest wall. Short snorts of air were all I could make out. My impulse was to jump out of my cocoon and race to the mist and embrace my dream. Instead, I remained like a statue, frantically searching for any sign of where the snorts were coming from.

After several moments of silence, I heard a horse coming from the end of the lake by the tree line.

"Oh my God!" I squealed out loud. "That's right where I was walking yesterday! Am I really awake? Is this really happening? Heart Horse, listen! It's really happening!"

The actual horse forms were hard to make out, but I could hear short snorts and smell the scent of horse wafting through the fog. I heard their movements, which sounded like an orchestra of familiar barn sounds playing not too far away.

I wondered how many there were. I wondered what colors they were. I wondered how long they'd stay. How long had they been there? A thousand questions swirled around in my head, but I was far too excited to make sense of any of them.

As I wiggled myself into a sitting position, cocooned tightly in my sleeping bag, my thoughts spun around in my mind.

Do they even know I'm here? I wondered. *Of course they do*, I answered myself. *They would smell a human from miles away. They probably have seen me, too, probably when I was dancing in the field of grass.*

The minutes felt like hours as the sun slowly lightened the darkness. I tried to sit as still as a statue, but I was so excited that I kept shifting position every few minutes. I knew they couldn't see me, but I was afraid they might vanish into the fog before I could catch sight of them.

Nothing else mattered at that moment—not my belly crying out for food, my bladder crying out for relief, or my chin crying out to be scratched. All that mattered was that soon they would appear, as if by magic, out of the fog.

Suddenly, a soft whinny broke the snorting song. Ever so slowly, I began to see their shapes and soft outlines. As if they had been sketched with a soft lead pencil on gray paper, the horse shapes appeared. A good-size group was gathering at the end of the lake. My eyes strained to see the fog-hidden colors, and all I could see were shades of gray.

I guessed that they were maybe a quarter mile away, which wasn't really that far considering they had been a lifetime away before that moment. Stretching my back, I sat up straight until I could see a bit further. Like watching a picture develop in a darkroom, the forms and colors were coming into focus, but the details remained hard to make out.

Despite my excitement, I could feel my body stiffen from being so still. With cold, unbendable fingers, I grasped the cocoon zipper and slowly unzipped my sleeping bag, freeing me from my confinement. I untangled my legs and stretched them out as far as I could, my eyes fixed straight ahead. Reaching around, I pulled my lumber jacket from where it had been squished into a pillow and wrapped it around my shoulders.

Lowering my eyelids for a moment, I pictured myself on one of the horses. I sat tall and strong on her back. Both my hands were wound around long knots of golden mane. We were one blended in form as I moved with her movement. Then we flew magically into a magical space made just for us in the mountain wall. We were Wind Horse and Spirit Horse finally united.

A gurgle of laughter shattered my fantasy flight, bringing me back to the present. Refocusing my eye on the emerging picture, I counted seven horses. There was a maple colored horse with a blonde mane, and a white one, as bright as snow. Most of them were shades of brown with odd white splashes around their noses or foreheads. One was a bit taller than the rest and didn't seem to be interested in breakfast like the others. I realized she was probably the leader.

She stood proudly like a masterpiece someone had just painted. She was creamy vanilla with splashes of chocolate brown on both sides. Her painter had flicked his brush at random intervals, providing such an interesting pattern I knew I would never forget her.

Her eyes focused on me. My eyes focused on her, both of us trying to determine if we could trust the other not to hurt us. I forced my eyes to look away in hopes of reassuring her that I was not threat.

With a loud snort and a shake of her withers, she dropped her head to the grass before her. Joy and relief surged through my heart. I could barely keep my squeal of delight inside. She hadn't fled.

Uncle Willy had been right all along. I'd found my wild horses. But instead of thundering into view, they had appeared when I least expected them, in a quiet and unassuming manner—just like life's most precious gifts.

It was exactly as Daryl had come into my life, I realized. Life's gifts have a way of coming to us in such unexpected moments and such unexpected ways. All I'd ever had to do was let it happen.

The painted one moved to the outside of the group as if keeping guard, still eating with only the occasional glance in my direction. The sun had opened in full bloom. The rays of heat wiped the ground clean of the remaining gray fog, and I could see them clearly. The leader was slowly making her way around the edges with a watchful eye. Behind her was a large horse, deep chestnut in color. By his antics, I could tell he was probably quite young. He kept trying to break out of the group, and the pale one, the leader, gave a short loud grunt and wedged him back each time.

I wondered how much movement I could make without scaring them away. Nature was calling me and my bladder was clenched in an unforgiving spasm. Rocking back and forth, I moved to all fours, like a dog, glancing up to see if they'd respond. The pale one gave me a sidelong look, stared for a moment, and returned to feeding. Moving back onto my haunches, I sat back. Swinging her head back and forth in small pendulum movements, she snapped off the blades of grass as I watched.

The rest of the herd paid no attention. They seemed to be content to follow her lead. Slowly, like a puppet being drawn up by strings, I stood upright. Still and silent, hands at my sides, I waited. Suddenly, they all jerked to attention and looked my way as if they had just noticed me for the first time.

Remembering my horse rules, I slowly moved my body sideways and stood quietly, waiting for their decision.

Please stay. Please stay. Please stay.

Holding my breath, Heart Horse, too, posed like a statue, and we waited. The pale one lowered her head and the others followed; they'd accepted me.

Now what? I wondered. I had to answer the call of nature or I'd burst. Fortunately, they were focused on their breakfast. Staying sideways to the herd, I unzipped my jeans and stepped over my backpack, lowering myself all in one motion. With a sigh of relief, my bladder let go.

Moving slowly, I returned to my sitting position on the other side of my pack in which I could concentrate on the scene before me. The morning air was drying the grass. My chin crust had tightened, pinching my skin. A breeze moved the stray hairs of my messy braid.

With the warm breeze came the beloved horse smells that I had longed to inhale for so long, filling my heart and soul with the memories and sustenance it so badly needed. Every few minutes the pale one looked my way, and then she returned to her meal. Heart Horse scampered with excitement each time she caught my eye.

As I watched them eat, I noticed they moved as one—one group, one family, moving together. Inch by inch they munched their way closer to the lake, closer to me.

How far will they come? I wondered.

My body was alive with energy. I felt in tune with the tiniest sensations of nature's world: the silky breeze, charged with energy and smells; the sun's rays penetrating the outer layer of my skin, warming even the deepest organ; and the sparkling lake that flashed in the corner of my eye. I watched the quivering mass of horseflesh chewing its way into my world. My body quivered with joy and excitement.

My breaths slowed to an even rhythm, and my eyes remained glued to the mare. Her chocolate brown swirls were splattered across a vanilla background, reminding me of a Salvador Dali painting. All that was missing were the melting clocks.

"We'll name her Dali," I told Heart Horse, and I felt him scampering joyfully in reply.

I had to sketch her, to record each chocolate swirl and paint spatter before she galloped away. I pulled the journal from its hiding place beneath my pack and opened it, pressing the pages flat with my palm.

What a magnificent creature she was. Without looking at the page directly, my pencil flew across the page, recording Dali's outline. Then, just as I pondered whether I should sketch in some apples for her to munch on, I realized I'd forgotten the bunch that I'd brought.

Reaching inside the open end of my pack, I felt around for the bag of apples until I found it. I decided to first reward my own belly with some morning nourishment. When I was done dining on my raw fruit, I had three apples left for the horses. All were rosy but beginning to show signs of travel. Brown spots were appearing on the once-perfect apples, giving them distinguishing Dali patches of their own.

Placing them in my lap, I examined each one. Gently I fingered the bruises, assessing the depth and flesh around the indentations.

The bruises weren't too deep, and I would have eaten them myself if I were hungry enough, so I figured they were fine for Dali and her family. But since there were only three apples, I would have to cut them up. If I cut them in quarters, I reasoned, I'd have twelve pieces of apple to share with the horses, which meant twelve chances to get close to them.

Placing the apples in my shirt, I pulled up the bottom hem, making a suitable container for carrying them. In slow motion I rose until I was upright. In silence I waited. After a moment, Dali swung her head up, looking in my direction. I froze, as still as a statue, my body sideways to her so I would not appear to be a threat.

Swiveling my head the same way Dali did, I looked toward the group. As I inched forward, they did the same. Sliding first my right foot then my left through the grass sideways, my eyes on the lake, I moved toward the horses at a barely perceptible glacial pace.

Suddenly, the young chestnut raised his glistening head and let out a loud whinny, shattering the silence just as he barreled through the group toward the lake. Dali immediately jumped into action and corralled him back into his place in the middle of the herd.

Like an exasperated mother, she shook her head, her beautiful mane flying across her back in ripples. With a deep growling snort, she butted his ribcage and returned to her position, all the while keeping a close guard on me, the bewildering intruder.

I didn't think she noticed that I had taken advantage of her distraction and moved closer, or maybe she chose not to let on. We were no more than a city block away from each other.

I felt Heart Horse galloping in excitement inside me and placed my hand over my heart, feeling the thud every few beats. One hand remained clutching the apples in my shirt container. As they rolled around I realized I'd have to sit to slice them into quarters. I silently lowered myself to my knees, spikes of grass jabbing sharply through my jeans.

My right hand wiggled deep into my pocket, and I pulled out my pocketknife, wincing at the memory of my beloved horse knife. Of everything I'd lost in my life, aside from Daryl, losing my horse knife hurt the most. It belonged here, with me, at this moment. But the ordinary pocketknife I'd picked up at a pawnshop in Toronto was going to have to do.

As I began slicing, Dali and her family watched in interest. With a flick of my wrist, the blade came out and stabbed into the first apple. Warm juice oozed onto my shirt, spreading apple blood in a Dali-patterned stain. I watched in fascination as the designs spread exactly like Dali's chocolate marks.

There is art in everything if you look closely, I thought.

With precision I created four pieces of identical apple morsels from each bruised and battered apple. By the time all three were sliced, the complete front of my shirt was warm and sticky with apple blood. Saliva pooled in my mouth in anticipation of how Dali would love her first bite.

Wiping my knife blade back and forth across my jeans, I dried it and returned the clean knife to my pocket, tightly gathering the pieces of apple in my shirt container.

As I unfolded my legs to a standing position, I slowly swiveled my head toward Dali. Our eyes met with sparks of electric recognition. My impulse was to look away. After all, that's what the rules said to do. However, my heart told me to look into her eyes. And as I did, I sent her a message of love and hope. Our moment lasted only seconds. She looked away first, but those few seconds were all the reward I needed. My heart pulsed with an intense stab of connection.

Every few moments one of the group lifted his or her head and stared in my direction, as I continued to slide ever so slowly toward them. After sensing that their leader was comfortable with my presence, one by one they returned to their breakfast of grass.

When I got as close as I possibly could, I stayed silent and unmoving. As I ran my tongue over my parched lips, I realized how thirsty, nervous, and afraid I had become. My mouth was so dry it was difficult to swallow, and I feared Dali would smell my growing fear. Droplets of sweat trickled down my back, and I felt an incomprehensible sense of anxiety as I stood so close to the wild horses of my childhood dreams.

It was time. I realized this might be my last chance before the herd ran off. Ignoring my fears and anxiety, I slowly slipped my hand into the shirt container and pulled out two pieces of warm apple flesh that were quickly turning soft and mushy.

Our eyes locked together as Dali watched to see what I was doing. I threw a slow-motion apple chunk in her direction. It landed just in front of her front hooves. With a gasp I sucked in a breath and waited for her reaction.

Dali swung her sweat-glistened neck around, first looking at me and then looking at my offering, so close to her hooves.

Please, please, please. Go ahead, Dali. Taste them. Please taste them. The silent wishes played several times in my mind, and I felt like a little girl so desperate to tame her wild pony. Dali lowered her head. With my head lowered, I watched her every move. Snorting greedily, she pushed the apple pieces with her snout, and in an instant, both pieces were gone.

She did it, Heart Horse! Oh my God, she did it! She did it! I had to seal my lips to keep the words in my head from flying out. I wanted to scream them out to the universe, but I couldn't. She had just told me, in horse language, that she trusted me, or at least, she trusted my gift to her.

A snort of thanks interrupted my excitement, and she wandered another few feet closer to the diamond lake. One by one, her family followed.

A slow motion horse dance began—me sliding one foot forward, the horse family one step away. Butterflies danced in my belly, and the corners of my lips cracked as they turned upward in a smile. I reached into my shirt basket and grabbed several apple pieces. As I pulled them out, I could see they had become egg-sized sticky chunks of brown apple flesh.

The air rippled with energy that seemed to flow from Dali's skin as her muscles flinched and flexed. The young chestnut was eager to see what was going on. With a burst of speed he broke from the group and raced around the edge of the lake, giddy with the taste of freedom.

I couldn't take my eyes off of him. He was so full of spirit and determination, truly an unfettered spirit of the mountains. I remembered how I had pranced naked through those same fields the day before, and I felt a secret bond. Dali watched her mischievous boy with one eye; the other eye she kept on me. His brief escape quickly over, he trotted back to his family. With a silence-shattering whinny, he returned to his place in the middle of the group.

I was amazed to watch how the horse family worked together as one. Dali was such a good mother. She intuitively understood the need for the occasional burst of freedom and had given him just enough time to express his wild side before urging him back into his family's protective circle.

I scattered all but two of the remaining apple pieces in the direction of the group and watched as Dali and her children gobbled up grass and apple.

What do you think, Heart Horse? Should I take the chance now? What if they run? Then it would be my fault that they left. On the other hand, if I don't try, I'll never know. I continued to imagine a dialogue with Heart Horse in my head, my only witness to this dream come true.

Inch by inch, I slid closer to the horses, stopping when Dali swung her head up and stared. The whites surrounding her chocolate eyes became luminescent with fear. I wanted her to know she shouldn't be afraid. I kept my body sideways, like the rules said, and my eyes slightly cast down but still within sight. Slowly, I pulled another apple piece from my shirt basket and reached out, holding it toward her like an offering, the soggy, sticky apple clinging to my palm.

"Come on, girl. You can do it. Come on. It's okay. Don't be afraid. You can do it." Every word brought me an inch closer to the group.

Suddenly, Dali swung her beautiful face toward me, and with a penetrating stare, she moved toward the lake. Away from me.

I thought I was just exhaling, but a soft, sad moan came from my parched throat as I threw the last pieces of apple toward Dali. She turned and I looked her straight in the eye, willing my words of gratitude straight from my soul to hers.

My watery eyes blinked like flashing lights as I tried to corral the tears and push them back inside. Sucking in horse energy, I watched in silence as my heart embraced the family heading toward the lake.

With a final wild swing of her head, Dali looked back at me, and I knew in that one instant that she was saying good-bye. In acknowledging her departure, she was letting me know that she'd accepted me. I had found my wild horse, and she would forever be mine, wherever she might be.

Dali turned away and charged into the lake, her family following behind. As they clambered onto the distant shoreline, I could hear the horses galloping over the rocks like a hundred Spanish castanets.

I breathed deeply for a few minutes, and then, with one final breath for Heart Horse, I knew my childhood was over. I may not have belonged to the family that had raised me, but I now knew that I belonged to the world, as wild and powerful as it was, and the world belonged to me.

I was ready to go home.

Epilogue

I wish I could tell you that after my trip to the Rockies I lived happily ever after. Recovering from abuse and addiction is never quite that easy, but I did grow and change with time and lots of hard work.

After returning to Toronto, I eventually stopped doing drugs and became a dedicated practitioner of Buddhism. I also returned to school, and despite my incarceration, I got my degree and had a rich and rewarding career as a registered nurse. I had an even richer and more rewarding life as a mother, raising a beautiful daughter who is now grown and has her own career as an artist.

In my memoir, *The Wall of Secrets*, I tell the story of returning to Belleville to care for my aging parents and facing the demons from my past.

Finally, after many long years of searching, I found and met the birth family I'd only dreamed of one day meeting and knowing. Having been ill for years with various symptoms of unknown origin, I was able, with genetic information, to put a name on what was affecting every aspect of my life. I was suffering with a rare mast cell disease, Systemic Mast Cell Activation Disorder, which had increased in severity throughout my life with each secret experienced or remembered. In *The Wall of Secrets*, I tell the story of this journey of unexpected twists and turns, a journey like nothing I would have imagined.

There is always hope, and if we dig deep enough, we will find the resilience to go forward.

May all beings have happiness and the causes of happiness; May all be free from sorrow and the causes of sorrow; May all never be separated from the sacred happiness which is sorrow-less; And may all live in equanimity, without too much attachment and too much aversion; And live believing in the equality of all that live.
—Traditional Buddhist Prayer

Recommended Reading

Benedict, Helen
Recovery: How to Survive Sexual Assault for Women, Men, Their Friends and Families
Columbia University Press, 1994

Brownmiller, Susan
Against Our Will: Men, Women, and Rape
Simon and Schuster, 1975

Bryant-Davis, Thelma, editor
Surviving Sexual Violence: A Guide to Recovery and Empowerment
Rowman & Littlefield Publishers, 2011

Cirocco, Grace
Take the Step, the Bridge Will Be There
HarperCollins Publishers, 1986

Denning, Patt, Jeannie Little, and Adina Glickman
Over the Influence: The Harm Reduction Guide for Managing Drugs and Alcohol
Guilford Press, 2004

Dupont, Robert L., MD

The Selfish Brain: Learning From Addiction
American Psychiatric Press, 2000

Follette, Victoria, PhD, and Jacqueline Pistorello, PhD

Finding Life Beyond Trauma
Guilford Press, 2007

Lifton, Betty Jean

Journey of the Adopted Self: A Quest for Wholeness
Basic Books, 1994
Lost and Found: The Adoption Experience
Harper & Row, 1988

Schiraldi, Glen

The Post-Traumatic Stress Disorder Sourcebook: A Guide to Healing, Recovery and Growth
Lowell House, 2000

Verrier, Nancy

The Primal Wound: Understanding the Adopted Child
Gateway Press, Inc., 2007
Coming Home to Self: The Adopted Child Grows Up
Gateway Press, Inc., 2003

Resources

National Drug Abuse Hotline: 1-800-662-4357

Break the Cycle: 1-888-988-8336

Love is Respect: 1-866-331-9475

National (Suicide) Hope-line Network: 1-800-784-2433

Kids Help Phone: 1-800-668-6868

Covenant House USA, National Runaway
Safe Line: 1-800-RUNAWAY

Crisis Shelter Covenant House Vancouver,
B.C. Canada: 1-877-6857474

Crisis Line USA: 1-800-273-8255 (TALK)

CPSIA information can be obtained at www.ICGtesting.com
Printed in the USA
LVOW12s1444280114

371322LV00002B/277/P